SAY GOODBYE TO GUILT

© By R. G. Condie

Plus: Curing the Common Cold
Dream Analysis
On Being Satisfied

With All Best Wishes
2004

AmErica House
Baltimore

First printing

ISBN: 1-58851-176-6
PUBLISHED BY AMERICA HOUSE BOOK PUBLISHERS
www.publishamerica.com
Baltimore

Printed in the United States of America

SAY GOODBYE TO GUILT

DEDICATION

To the memory of Bill Tummon.

He was my warm friend and

enthusiastic encourager.

R. G. Condie

INTRODUCTION

This book is not for clods. They don't need it. Clods don't develop emotional problems because their unidimensional approach to living is uncomplicated.

For a really good neurosis you require imagination, intelligence, and the ability to see many sides of a situation or condition. It also helps to have sensitivity, awareness, and the capacity to conceptualize. By this I am not implying that to be intelligent, sensitive, and aware is a guarantee of neurotic problems: not so. However, the simple premise of this book is: if you have within you the intelligence and sensitivity to get yourself emotionally screwed up, you also have the intellectual capacity to unscrew yourself.

Surprisingly, most people wouldn't mind being neurotic, except that it gets in the way of relationships with other people. Their solution is to seek ways to change themselves, a monumental task when it is the natural human being that needs changing. This book is not intended to change what you are. It is not even designed to change what you do, or what you believe just for the sake of change. What I do hope to give you here is another way of looking at yourself, of assessing what and who you are and how you became what you are. As a side benefit, the process will restore to your use some of the energy you presently use fighting yourself. If I can do this, all other things are possible, including change, if you still perceive that to be a benefit to you.

What follows is the presentation of a series of concepts for your consideration. The assumption is that you are not a clod but more likely are sufficiently bright to put these concepts to work for you, in your own environment, and under your own conditions. Please take them as concepts. Roll them around in your mind for a while. When you see a way they apply to you, put them to work right away. Should you question at first, play with them for a little while. Bounce them back and forth amongst your friends and relatives. Try them on for size before discarding them lightly. Try them as though you did agree with them and see how valid they can become for you. See how they work. I can assure you that they have worked for all kinds of people in all kinds of circumstances, for over a quarter century of use.

I realize that some take a little patient practise, so don't get hung up on any single concept. Let each simmer while you collect the others so you have a total package with which to work. I firmly believe that you will enjoy the total results as so many others have before you.

CHAPTER 1
There is No Such Thing as Altruism

Basic to the comprehension and understanding of the human animal is a simple-sounding concept. There is no such thing as altruism. Regardless of who or what else benefits from our actions, we always perceive a personal benefit from our actions; in this I would also include actively doing nothing when there is stimulus for doing something. It follows from this that, when we find ourselves doing something seemingly detrimental to ourselves or to our best interest, somewhere in the process we see a personal gain. Bearing in mind that avoidance of what we find unpleasant for us is in fact a gain, we find an effective tool for evaluating all our actions and lack of actions. When you find within yourself or your conduct that which is incomprehensible, ask yourself "What do I gain from this?" and you will find your explanation. This will be your explanation but not necessarily mine or anyone else's.

Also following from recognition of this basic premise comes the awareness that there can never be an illogical human act. Regardless of how seemingly incomprehensible our action may appear to others or even ourselves, there is always a traceable chain of logic. When our actions seem detrimental, this chain of logic usually leads to some miscalculation of facts or factors, but it does lead logically, and, most important, it can be traced.

I like to use the story about a young man who, every Tuesday afternoon at four o'clock, jumps in front of a bus at the northeast corner of Yonge and Eglinton in Toronto. This would appear to be obviously self-destructive behavior. To help trace the logic we use a standard Gestalt Therapy concept that tells us that we cannot see any situation without seeing it against the background of that situation. Nothing can be seen standing alone. It must be viewed in the total context of its background. The young man's actions are a case in point.

The background for this story is that at four o'clock every Tuesday afternoon, a sweet young woman walks her pet tiger on the northeast corner of Yonge and Eglinton. The tiger hates our young man's guts. Our young man does not actually jump in front of buses. He jumps away from an angry tiger.

We can all see the immediate benefit of getting away from an angry tiger, even if it means risking a jump in front of a bus that may or may not stop. Given the background, we can all see the logic behind our young man's actions when he finds himself with only these two choices. Key to complete understanding is a review of the logic that finds him on that same corner, at that same time every week.

Before we can change our young man's actions, we must understand his reason (gain) for being in harm's way every week. He has three other corners from which to choose at this one intersection alone. He has twenty-three other hours of every Tuesday when, if need be, he could use the northeast corner. What does he gain from repeatedly choosing this risk? Does he have an even bigger tiger inside him? Is he afraid of appearing weak if he picks another time or another place? Has he convinced himself that it's up to the young lady with the tiger to make alternate choices, or even that the bus could pick another route since he got there first? Is it possible his self-esteem would be strained if he admitted that his choice of time and place was a 'mistake' even though he may have originally been unaware of the schedules of both bus and beast?

I am sure all my readers can add their own conceivable permutations, combinations, and variables, to guess what goes into our young man's thinking. While only he can tell us for certain, I am sure you can identify with some of his difficulties. Take a look at some of your own seemingly self-destructive behavior in the light of this basic concept. We always do that which we perceive to be of the most benefit to us, regardless of who else may also benefit.

Over the many years I have worked with people, this concept engenders the most rigid of all resistance. No other notion, theory, or philosophical idea prompts as much protest. Everyone has his or her own example of true altruism. I've had charity of all types presented as altruism, yet none can deny the pleasure we all enjoy internally from being charitable. One young lady was insistent that she was altruistic. Whenever a friend, relative, or acquaintance asked her to do something, she always did it, whether she really wanted to or not. When I asked her if she was capable of saying no, she eventually realized that she was both emotionally incapable of saying no and bitterly resented being constantly put upon by those who knew that she couldn't say no.

I know that for anyone to agree that there is no altruism is hard, if for no other reason than that we must then recognize that we never really get anything for nothing from others. They always perceive a benefit. But remember, sometimes that benefit is the pleasure of seeing our reaction or our own pleasure, so that what is benefit to them may not always be a negative to us.

If you must search for some evidence of altruism, please search only within your own experience. Only you can be sure of the complete motivation within you and your actions. Let others speak for themselves and from their experience.

Once you are convinced, or even just to a point where you can agree that it is possibly true, I can go on to show you how frustration need never be a factor in your life again. It is a simple further step. Frustrate is defined as "to prevent from obtaining a purpose." When we always gain from our actions, we are always doing what we want to do. I enjoy recognizing that since I always do what I want to do, I can never be frustrated.

Let me use another story as an example. I'm driving along a city street, approximately two minutes away from my destination where I have, for me, an extremely important appointment. Suddenly the light turns red in front of me, and, at the same time, I notice the police car idling at the intersection. If I obey the stoplight, I'll be late for my appointment. If I run the light, the police will surely stop me, with again the equal certainty that I will be late. Regardless of what I do at this point in time, I cannot make my important meeting in time. The potential for frustration is great.

If it weren't for that damn light, I could have made it. If it weren't for that damn cop, I could have run the light and made it, but no, he had to be there waiting when I didn't need him. If it weren't for the damn meeting, I wouldn't have any of these hassles. If I didn't make a fetish of being punctual, it wouldn't matter to me, and if I hadn't been conscientious in completing my last appointment, I wouldn't be in this bind now. Instead, I'm potentially frustrated at every turn, even by myself.

If I choose to, I can frustrate myself, judge myself, find myself guilty, and punish myself with even more frustration. It just might impress the person I'm meeting if he can see how really guilty and frustrated I feel. As my father would say, "It's a mug's game." It is self-destructive, unrealistic, dishonest, and totally unnecessary. Let's examine this situation thoroughly in the context that I benefit from everything I do and find what is my most pleasant option or options.

Would I like to live in a city, or anywhere for that matter, without police protection? I think not. Would I like to drive anywhere without traffic controls? I know not. At the same time these controls are "forcing" me to do this, that, and the next thing, I'm being protected as others are equally restricted. Would I like to be without appointments with their implicit need for me? Would I like to be without the awareness of time and the order it brings into my existence? Can I perceive of any rational situation where I would choose to live in anarchy? No, No, and again, No!

Frustration ceases to be part of everyone's life when there is recognition that all our life situations stem from, and are part of choices we make, always having as their motivation, some advantage for ourselves.

My meeting with the stoplight cannot be frustrating. The same holds true for other life problems where we seem to be forced into actions or decisions we don't want to do or make. All situations can be traced back to our choice. As Fritz Perls loved to observe, sometimes our choice is between chicken shit and elephant shit, but we do have the choice. An honest analysis always shows us that the choice to be where elephants abound was our's in the first place. So, as adults, even the saddest and seemingly restrictive choices can be traced and found to result from other choices made earlier, all of them our own, all made with our best interest at heart, and all with a built-in benefit to us.

Take this concept and live with it. Play with it. Analyze as many situations as you like. Bounce it off your friends and relatives. Let them try to provide examples of altruism from their own personal experience, but not from hearsay. As so many others have found before you, you will find that this concept holds true in every case, without exception. Accept this concept only after you yourself have run sufficient tests to be completely convinced. Why? Because my next concept contends that, once convinced, we can begin to comprehend the motive behind all our actions, and all the actions of others. There will be no need to make those total re-examinations of every situation, which take so much time and effort. You will have taken a major step toward understanding all people, including yourself. You will never again need to second-guess either yourself or any of your actions regardless of outcome. You will know that somehow, some way, your actions were motivated by a perceived benefit to you. When anyone questions your actions, and yes, that includes yourself, you can now simply and accurately state, "I did it because I chose to do it." This is more than enough of an answer for you or anyone else, as you will discover in future chapters.

Since you have read this far, I assume we agree that you are one of the bright ones. With this knowledge and armed with our first two concepts, we can now recognize that any situation where we apparently failed can never be considered a failure because we only do what we want to do. Simply because we are certain that we have a personally perceived pay-off for every action, it follows that any "failure" must in reality be our success in completing a gainful failure.

Contradictory, confusing, but conclusively reality. When someone works so hard at failing, how can he or she or you be called anything but successful? Find your tiger and you may come to equally enjoy a successful success.

One final note. In assessing whether there is or is not some altruism in human acts, avoid the trap of using someone else as an example. Because we can never know everything that goes into anyone else's decision to act, we can be trapped into thinking they really are altruistic. Once we accept that idea, there is a risk that we will see them as somehow better people than we are. Instead, know yourself and you know every man. Be yourself and you can hold your head high in any company. Especially when you lack the time to investigate all the facts, be fair enough to avoid any ill-formed opinions. You have a personal gain for all that you do. Others have a gain for all that they do. You are the equal of anyone until you prove otherwise.

CHAPTER 2
Liking Yourself

Do you really like yourself? Don't be coy or shy. This is just between us. If you like yourself, can we go one step further? Do you love yourself? You may ask, does it really matter? It certainly does, and let me show you why.

Let's assume we meet, are of the "proper" genders to satisfy our acceptable standards for friendship, then watch the disaster our relationship becomes if I have a low opinion of myself: Not even a bottom of the scale personal dislike of myself: All it takes is a low appraisal of my self-worth.

I see you, I meet you, and I like you. There is something about you I find attractive, appealing, or both. I'm immediately aware that here is someone with qualities I value, and who can be of value to me. Just as quickly I will become aware of the great difficulty I have in letting you see that I place a high value on you, or what I perceive to be you. I may even quickly blot from my own perception that fact that I am interested in you.

I will be so busy looking at me and wondering what you think of me, that all my natural responses will be drowned in a sea of self-consciousness. (For the record. Self-consciousness can be cured simply by looking at others and asking yourself, "I wonder what I think of them.") Instead, I will become a little bit awkward, a little bit reticent, and I will probably appear a little bit phoney, which I will be.

However, if you are the person I perceive you to be, i.e., someone of value, you will probably recognize my shy, reticent, self-conscious behavior as all too typical of the response you receive from many other people. In spite of this, and possibly even because of this, you may take the time to look and find something in me that is of value to you.

And so begins the faltering process of "getting to know each other." I find in you someone with whom I wish to spend my time, share my thoughts, and so as the weeks go by it becomes apparent we are becoming friends. Because I value myself so little, I will probably try to be an exceptionally good friend in the things I do and take an extra interest in you and what you do and how you feel. In short, I will compensate for the failings I know I have, by making a special effort to be a good friend on the surface.

As long as our relationship remains on this plane, there are no real problems. I know I'm getting much more out of you than you could possibly get out of me, but that's all right. I'm used to people watching me and recognizing this.

All of a sudden one day our relationship takes a dramatic turn. You say you like me! But I know I'm not likeable. You have just presented me with a terrible question. Are you a liar, or are you just blind?? Because I perceive myself to be of little value, I can't possibly accept that you like me. Because I like you, I don't want to believe you're a liar, and to discover that this person I like so much is a liar would shake what little self-confidence I have left. So I'll devise a few little tests to see if you really are a liar or not. Assuming you pass my little tests, which I will choose to make simple hoping you will pass them, I will come to the conclusion that you are simply blind.

By saying you like me, you have added a new dimension to our relationship. Fritz Perls used to say, "Anxiety increases proportionately with the distance in our thinking between the here and now, and our thinking of the future." How true that statement is in this case.

You have said you like me. Now I know you are blind. When can I expect the scales to drop from your eyes? When will you unexpectedly see me as I really am? You will not only not like me anymore, but in your disappointment you will probably leave and I will never see you again. Well, that has happened to me before and will probably happen to me again. In the meantime, since I still find you of value, I'll continue to associate with you, and be your friend, but! I won't be quite as attentive as before. I won't work quite as hard at being a friend, and you may even notice it. You may even wonder if, now you have committed yourself and said you like me, I am taking you for granted. I know that's not true, but I may let you believe it because I would rather that be the reason you start liking me less, instead of because you have really seen me for what I am. Someone of little value.

If, in spite of all this our relationship continues to grow, and you still seem disinclined to see me as I see myself, my anxiety must continue to grow accordingly. You are becoming more valuable to me. My potential loss is increasing. Sooner or later you've got to see me as I am. And so I'll start another round of testing. I'll keep them little to start with. Something you have requested and I have agreed to, I'll forget. When you mention it, all apologetically I rush out to do what I had agreed to do. I may even do something extra because I really don't want to lose you. But it is important that you see me for what I am.

If this ploy doesn't work, I'll try not being available for several nights. This is a super combination of self-punishment and showing you. I won't give any explanation except that I have something else to do. If pressed for explanations, it can be that I need to get my hair cut. I need to take my mother shopping, whether I have for the last ten years of not. I've got work to do for my boss, or a client. All very reasonable, but the fact remains I am not going to be available when you would like me to be with you.

If this tactic simply upsets you and doesn't force you to see me as I really am, I'll probably be so guilty that, for the next little while, I'll make a special effort to be more like the person I was before you said you liked me. Now you have the old me to contend with, the one you grew to like in the first place. You may put my testing down as many things except what they really were: Maybe momentary aberrations, bad moods, difficulties in other parts of my life that you may even wish to share. At this point in time our relationship can either proceed to die as I expect, or grow out of this into the final stages. Either way, the end is never in doubt. Our relationship will never survive my insecurities. It cannot survive my perceived lack of self-worth.

If, wonder of wonders, you now say that you love me, our entire relationship is doomed. You may extend it for months, or even years, but just as surely as if you took me out and drowned me, you doom it. Because I now have so much time invested in you, both to be with you, and to show you what I am, I probably am in love with you, and have been for some time. I have even probably been hoping you love me because love is blind, and that above all else is what I need in a lover. Someone who is blind!

But now you are faced with someone who shows all the classic symptoms of schizophrenia. I am schizophrenic where you are concerned. Possibly not clinically so, but just look at it from my point of view. Here I have someone I value and love. You say you love me. Yet I know I am not even likeable, much less lovable. My inclination will be to cling to you, to try to be what you perceive me to be. But tearing me from the other side will be the knowledge that you can't possibly stay blind forever. At those moments when I want you most with me, my instincts will be screaming at me to run from you. "Don't get committed," I'll tell myself. "The break-up pain will be too great." I don't want you being so nice to me. That's just going to make our final parting even harder.

The better friend and better lover you become, the more disturbed I'll become. Even you will begin to notice my flashes of anger in your direction, and for reasons you just can't fathom. Of course I'm angry! Here I am, totally convinced our relationship must eventually break up, and you're being so damned nice it's just making it harder and harder. You'll notice the beginnings of resentment. I'll notice you're baffled by it and I won't be able to explain to you because that would hasten the end. Eventually I will be emotionally incapable of withstanding the contrast between my warm pleasure in your company, and my expected desolation when you leave.

If you persist in not seeing me for what I know I am and don't leave me, you confront me with the most agonizing of decisions. I can't stand waiting for you to leave. The suspense is killing me. If you don't leave, I will. I have to.

In some relationships this parting procedure may be total and final the first time. In others there may be reconciliations and the eventual end may be delayed. The result remains inevitable. Either I drive you away, or run away myself. I cause the destruction of something of value to you and something of exceptional value to

16

me, all because I am not of sufficient value to me. The final irony in this tragedy in human relations is that my perception of self is all too often ill-advised, ill-founded, and inaccurate.

The tortured trail that leads us to this sad state in our self-appraisal may vary in the facts behind it and in the intensity from one individual to another. In twenty-five years of involvement in psychotherapy, the path seems all too similar. The stories seem all too familiar. I have also discovered there are three basic laws in human relationships, particularly in one-to-one situations.

Like yourself, or no one else can risk it.

Accept yourself, or no one else can afford to.

Love yourself, or no one else can hope to.

My intention and expectation in writing this book are to change the way you perceive yourself, and the way that you judge yourself, all without changing you. The basic "you" will, I hope, remain the same while you go on to gain new insights into that basic "you" and recognize the traps into which you have fallen or been led that destroy your awareness of your own value.

You will be the same, but if I do my job, when you finish this book you will have learned how to live with yourself and like it. You will Say Goodbye To Guilt.

CHAPTER 3
JUDGING YOURSELF

How do you see yourself? How clearly do you see yourself? How realistically do you evaluate what you perceive yourself to be? Let's find out.

Bisect a large sheet of paper so that you have two long columns. In the right-hand column, print the headings, Assets, Positive Qualities, Pluses, and Things I Like About Myself. Head the left-hand column Liabilities, Negative Qualities, Minuses, and Things I Don't Like About Myself.

Next, without checking future instructions, write down as quickly and as honestly as you can, everything you know about yourself into the columns in which they apply. Now set your page or pages aside for a few moments. Just let them sit there.

Ready to go again? OK. Review your lists and add anything you may have remembered, again set your list aside for a further few moments. When you're ready we'll go on.

LIST # 1

❏ MINUSES ❏ LIABILITIES ❏ NEGATIVE QUALITIES ❏ THINGS I DON'T LIKE ABOUT MYSELF	❏ PLUSES ❏ ASSETS ❏ POSITIVE QUALITIES ❏ THINGS I LIKE ABOUT MYSELF

Assuming you have been honest with yourself, the list now in front of you is a composite picture of the "you" that other people are being asked to accept, reject, or tolerate. Take a totally honest look at the whole picture: All the pluses and all the minuses. As a totality, would you want this person for a friend?

In all my years of working with people, I have never seen a list without some pluses. There has always been something of value to me in the total, and often an asset that alone and in itself tips my scales toward acceptance. All I ask is that someone let me see what they are, so that I at least have a chance to choose.

Take two more large sheets of paper, heading one exactly the same as your first. Head the second: Physical attributes that are me, either acceptable, unacceptable, or changeable with operation. Review your first completed list and remove all comments on your physical characteristics. These are written onto your new "Physical" list. Set this list aside for the moment. We don't need it for this exercise.

Take the items remaining on your original list, and, expressing them more concisely, preferably in one word, write them onto your new FINAL LIST # 3. For example, if your minus list shows "I wouldn't let my sister wear my new dress first to go to a party. I know she really wanted to but she gets sloppy when she drinks," substitute a single word like "selfish" or "prudent," and put it on your new list. Do the same for any other lengthy explanations, substituting wherever possible a single word that expresses the meaning clearly.

Physical attributes, Plus or minus. These are you. They can be acceptable or unacceptable or changeable by operation or cosmetics.

List them and forget them for now.

LIST # 2

FINAL LIST # 3

❏ LIABILITIES ❏ MINUSES ❏ NEGATIVES	❏ ASSETS ❏ PLUSES ❏ POSITIVES

Don't be surprised when your list becomes shorter because a number of the items on your first list may boil down to the same thing on your final list. Again, take a real and honest look at the list in front of you now. Fat or thin, tall or short, green or purple, would you want this person for a friend?

22

Now you have your final list. Now we can start to have some real fun. By now the final list in front of you is a concise but complete picture of you, as you see yourself at this minute. It is also in all probability the list by which you assess yourself as valuable or not valuable to yourself and others. Unless you are totally unique to my experience, your list will show a picture so full of distortions that we can begin the process of rebuilding your self-esteem in the next few pages. Let's see what happens when we look closely.

Now, review every single trait that you have on your list, both plus and minus, to see which could be equally plus or minus depending on the background against which we view them. It is rare in my experience to find a list without the word "sensitive" or its equivalent. The only question is always, "On which side will I find it?" Think about it for a while. If **your** sensitive is on the plus side, you probably have recently experienced a pleasant situation where your enjoyment was heightened by your sensitivity. On the other hand, if you have just been hurt, we will find **your** sensitive listed as a negative. Like so many other of life's conditions, your traits don't make sense by themselves, but only as we see them against a background.

Find all the characteristics on your list that can be both pleasant and unpleasant for you, depending on the situation or circumstances in which they occur. Clearly mark each with an asterisk to remind yourself that regardless of which side you have placed them today, these are really all assets in a multifaceted human being, and in themselves can never be detrimental or demeaning. In reality, the simple fact that they are you and in you is a large plus! Let that one simmer for a while.

Next, take all the items on one side of your list, and match them to the items on the other side of your list that are the same thing. Does your list show a + **determined**, and a - **stubborn**? They are the same thing. If you are aggressively plowing ahead in my direction, you are determined. When everything remains the same except you choose the opposite direction to mine, of course you must be stubborn. Draw a circle around each word, then draw a connecting line between them to remind yourself again that here is a plus and a minus that cancel each other out, leaving only a valuable capacity.

Does your list show + sensitivity, and - easily hurt? These too are the same thing. Another set of connected circles please.

Honest	=	tactless
Aggressive	=	pushy
Trusting	=	naive
Flexible	=	inconsistent
Generous (or giving)	=	soft touch
Open-minded	=	easily swayed
Understanding	=	emotional push-over
Firm values	=	opinionated
Stand for beliefs could	=	opinionated/argumentative/or belligerent and so on, and, so on and so on.

Notice how often one item on one side connects with more than one item on the other side. Circle and connect them all.

Now, take another look at your lists and see how many items on your total list must be flat contradictions. Some may be on the same side, and others opposite. Do you show both sensitive and heartless? Firm and flexible? Understanding and argumentative? Pleasant and miserable? Put a square or a different-colored circle around each and connect these pairs as a further reminder that these too cancel each other out as either pluses or minuses and remain only as valuable traits.

Be reasonable! How many of the items on your lists is anything more or less than the valuable human attribute of a many-sided human being? In fact, is there anything at all on your lists that fails to qualify as valuable when beneficially used by you and those in your environment? I doubt it.

Notice what the real difference is between stubborn and

determined. If you're going my way I applaud your determination. Go against me and I will castigate you with the label of stubborn. The exact same human act or characteristic finds itself on opposite side of **your** list depending on my judgement of its benefits to **me**, not you. When you don't give me what I want selfishly from you, I'll give you a **selfish** for your minus list. When I get what I want, I'll give you a **generous** for your plus list. Can you see how I might have figured out that calling you generous was cheaper for me, than paying for what I want?

When you tune into my needs or wants without my asking, I give you a **sensitive** for your plus list. But if you should become upset when my wants become silent demands, I can either risk having to pay in some way for what I want, or whip you back into line with a **too easily hurt**, or **selfish** for your minus list.

What do all these adjectives on your list have potentially in common? They can be judgements. Laid-on, or self-induced, they can be judgements with all the upset and discomfort this induces. Look long and hard at your lists. How many items are genuine objective self-appraisal, and how many are judgements all too often imposed on your self-esteem by someone like me who has discovered that you can be controlled by guilt? Don't believe it? Think I'm exaggerating?

Watch!

I want to go from Toronto to Buffalo. I can buy a ticket on a plane, a bus, or a train. I can rent or buy a car, rent a limousine, or call a cab. In reviewing all my options I find they all have one sad common denominator. I have to pay.

Just as this reality is hitting home, I notice you and happily remember that you have a car. What could be simpler? I'll get you to drive me. While we are exchanging the usual pleasantries, I go over in my mind all the things that I have to offer you as inducement for driving me to Buffalo. Sad reality number two hits home. In either the same or differing ways, I must either end up paying for my trip in cash, or offering something of value as payment to you. This is what I wanted to avoid in the first place. I want a better (read that as cheaper) way to get what I want.

I know! I'll make you feel guilty. First I build you up. "I know you are a generous, understanding, and good friend. A good, understanding, and generous friend couldn't possibly see me not getting to Buffalo." We let that one sink in for a while. Now the longer you take to decide to drive me to Buffalo, the more you begin to look like a cheap, unfeeling, poor friend. I won't even have to pass judgement on you. You'll do it yourself for me. Having judged yourself, found yourself guilty and "realized" that you deserve punishment, all that's left for me to do is to let you drive me to Buffalo for free, partly as punishment, and partly to expiate your guilt.

If that were the end of it, all you would be out would be the expense in time, energy, and gasoline needed to drive me to Buffalo. Unfortunately, the more likely reality is that you will also be left with the thought that you are basically a selfish, thoughtless, and poor friend indeed (a thought I may choose to nurture against some future personal need.)

There has to be a better way. There has to be a happier way. There is. First, let's examine judgement.

CHAPTER 4
JUDGEMENT

Judgement. How many of the negatives that we see in ourselves are really judgements? How many are the ways in which we use judgement to devalue our opinion of ourselves? And most cruelly, how often are these self-judgements totally contradictory, as we have seen in the previous chapter? I am certain you have begun to observe in the last chapter the obviously large role that judgement plays in our critical assessment of self. I am firmly convinced that learning to at least cope, if not live, with judgements is absolutely crucial for mental equanimity.

Let me define judgement as I most often encounter the beast. An opinion is just that, and only slightly stronger than an impression. Add a list of facts to the opinion/belief, and we have an assessment. Take either or both, compare it to an ideal, whether our, mine, your, or anyone's conception of "society's," then add an understood penalty clause when we fall short, and you have the "judgement" I most often encounter.

The penalty requires that fault or guilt be established, and punishment must then follow. Take this as a guarantee. Open the Pandora's box of judgement and you open yourself to the whole guilt/fault/blame complex and almost constant exposure to a need for punishment. The only open question is whether we would rather punish ourselves, or be punished by others. Put the book down for a few moments and ask yourself, "Would I rather punish myself, or leave it in the hands of someone or something else?" Come to grips with what you truly believe.

In my estimation, the classic example of the judgement/sentencing/punishment cycle is most evident in small children. Have you ever watched when a small child is tempted with a bowl of candies or cookies, all well within reach on a low table, but is warned not to touch? Small boys, particularly those who have not been totally broken and repressed, will reach out, steal a goody, slap their own hand, intone "bad boy!" and then look up, convinced that the situation is now finished.

Can you see a little bit of you in our little boy? Are you among the vast majority in my experience who punish themselves rather than risk losing control of the process to some outside force? That's right. When you think about it, we can control our own punishment and thus control both situation and severity. We can be the arbiter of how much or how little pain and discomfort a particular guilt requires. It is true that most people seek to have control over their lives, including punishment, whenever possible.

However, if we are unable or unwilling to complete the judgement/punishment cycle ourselves, and equally unwilling to leave the job to others, the situation remains incomplete and unfinished. These unfinished situations must then be carried with us like a yoke around our shoulders and a lump on our minds that never erodes or disappears.

We discovered an amazing example of this in our pet terrier Taffy. Wire-haired Terriers are strong willed and Taffy was no exception, but she did have one unfortunate physical problem. Her bladder and kidneys were weak. We learned very quickly that even as an adult animal, Taffy could not hold her bladder for more than six hours. She would often try, but the back up of poisons in her system made her so physically ill that she became unstable on her feet and quite sadly disoriented until relieved. With both my wife and myself busy with demanding jobs, it was often necessary for us to be unexpectedly away from the house for over six hours. Once Taffy had been trained to go outside every time, we couldn't establish an inside alternative she would use. As a result, when we came home we would find either a sick little animal, or a mess on the floor and a sad dog.

The first few times we found a puddle, we were full of sympathy for the poor little animal and tried to reassure her that she was a "good dog" and that we did not believe it was her fault in any way. It didn't work. Taffy's barometer of moods, her tail, stayed down despite our repeated assurances that all was OK. Her unhappy state would often last for days until we stumbled on the answer quite by accident. Arriving home one night much later than expected, we discovered a puddle, but not on the easily cleaned tile

28

kitchen floor. It was on our favorite throw rug. While we were examining the damage and wondering if a rescue was possible, Taffy came to us in her usual down-tailed condition, even though she was bright enough to sense we were upset with her. In a fit of what I choose to consider as understandable pique, one of us swatted her with the handful of mail we had just picked up and called her a bad dog for good measure. To our amazement, up came the tail and we were presented with a happy playful dog! A crime had been committed, and the anticipated punishment delivered. The situation was now complete in Taffy's mind, so our little dog was relieved and happy again.

Unlike you and I, Taffy had no conception of self-punishment. When she broke one of our rules, she was totally dependent on us to complete the cycle by providing punishment. There is one thing we too often have in common with Taffy. Even when there is no reason for either judgement or punishment, when we anticipate them, they have to be applied to complete the situation and the cycle.

I wonder how often you stand in judgement of yourself, where a court of law might see extenuating circumstances, or at least some doubt that would lead to a verdict of not guilty. When we insist on controlling the whole process to ensure our control of the punishment just in case, we often drag ourselves through the entire process needlessly.

This type of habit pattern can become ingrained. When it does, we see that sort of behavior in our group that I am sure you have noticed socially. There is the individual who always laughs when talked to, and who prefaces every personal comment with a laugh or giggle. He has recognized that when someone laughs at him, it is a form of judgement. The solution, which always leaves him in control of the situation, is to always laugh first. You can't be laughed at when you're laughing too. To avoid any external judgement, all you have to do is judge yourself first. It works, but at what a price!

Look at what is required, and what you have provided. You have set up a complete, portable, and ever-present court system.

You have a judge: Yourself. You have a diligent prosecutor: Yourself. You have the ever-present, all-seeing prosecution eyewitness: Yourself. You have a built-in executioner and/or purveyor of punishment: Yourself. Finally, you have the victim: Also often yourself. But what you don't have and rarely provide is a defense attorney. Obviously you can't be both prosecutor and defender. It's all very logical, all very complete, and unquestionably all very effective, once you have had a chance to develop the techniques.

Just before we go on, I would like to check the accuracy and completeness of your memory. Let's go back in time, just five minutes. What exactly were you doing exactly five minutes ago? Were you standing or sitting? What exactly were you thinking? Were all the parts of your body comfortable? Were you warm? Were you tense? What was your exact emotional state? What emotion-altering colors were in your field of vision? What was happening in your immediate environment? Were there any distractions from people, pets, or passing planes? Was the radio on? the stereo? or the T.V.? If so, what exactly was playing or happening exactly five minutes ago?

Was your body in an open position, with feet and arms apart indicating an openness of mind exactly five minutes ago? Or were your arms or feet, or fingers, or toes crossed? Did you have a hand over your ear so you wouldn't hear something? Did you have a hand over your mouth so you wouldn't say something? Were you coughing because you wanted to respond to what you were reading, thinking, or hearing, but repressed yourself? Were you comfortable with what you were doing, understanding what you were seeing, or puzzled?

If you can remember even one tenth of the answers to my questions, you are a uniquely aware individual with an extremely retentive memory. It is far more like that you can't exactly remember any of the details of anything that was happening to you just five short minutes ago. Remember this fact.

Let's return to your own little internal court for a few moments. You are the prosecutor. You are the executioner. You are usually the only eyewitness. But most important: You are the judge. Are you a fair and impartial judge? Even if never before, could you at this moment become a reasonable and impartial judge? Now let me be that defense attorney who is usually missing from your private courtroom.

Your Honor! Today we have in the dock an habitual criminal. Rarely an hour, much less a day, goes by without this villain needing to appear before you. Time after time you have brought him to trial and found him wanting. Time after time you have found him guilty, all too often of the same offenses. Time after time you have passed judgement, until by now his sentences are overlapping, and still he keeps coming back. He doesn't even put up a reasonable defense any more because, like you, he all too often laughingly assumes his guilt before he even enters the courtroom.

And yet . . . Something else is the same in every trial. In every case we have the same witness. An eyewitness: A witness always on the scene. And Damn it, Your Honor, in every case we have a witness who we have just proven cannot remember clearly and completely what happened a mere five minutes ago! By all that is reasonable and all that is just, by every tenet of fair play we have ever considered, I ask you, how are we able to contemplate, much less accept the evidence of this so-called witness? One who vaguely remembers what happens, one who vaguely recollects what was happening in the background, one who has no firm retention of the emotional processes that led to the actions or reactions of the accused, or for that matter, any other extenuating circumstances. This solitary witness has only the vaguest retrospection of the actions of the accused, and that in some vague time frame.

Even if we brought in an outside witness, when we review his testimony based on our experiment with this witness, is there any reason to believe the testimony would be more complete? On the contrary, it is far more likely given their own small interest in themselves, and their subjective viewpoint, their memory of the actions and behavior of the accused will be even less accurate than those of this pitiful excuse for a witness whom we see here every day. On another point I ask you what kind of court do we have here that, day by day, minute by minute, insists that a defendant must testify against himself? There is no parallel in any other fair legal system. No other fair legal system would tolerate not just double jeopardy, but multiple jeopardy, for every offense, however minor.

I ask you again, Your Honor, is there anyone else in the world upon whom you would pass judgment for one tenth of the indictments of this defendant? Would you contemplate, much less accept, the evidence of such an ill-advised witness? And if anyone else in this world were brought before your court, would your sentences be so harsh? I sincerely doubt it.

You're the judge. Tell me. Are you being fair? Are you being reasonable? Are you being even mildly realistic? I suspect the answer is no in every case. And if, as I suspect, that answer is no, that triggers the obvious question, "If I'm so bright and I'm so logical, how in hell did I get myself in such a mess?" Be aware that this is the type of logic that keeps our young friend jumping into front of buses to get away from tigers. The progression may be logical, but some of the facts could stand re-examination.

As to your being bright, you damn well have to be bright to keep this courtroom in session twenty-four hours a day and still continue to function in some semblance of rational fashion in your day-to-day life.

Add to your mental courtroom the complexities of continually meting out punishment in one form or another. Add to this whole process, the energy loss from fighting yourself when you avoid a situation that you recognize will have you back in your private court. And finally, let's face it. If your instincts or desires have you wishing to go in one direction with twenty percent of your energy, it requires an equal restraining twenty percent just to stand still. In reality, if you are moving at all it's amazing. It's also highly complimentary to the mental processes that help you keep all these mental balls juggling at the same time.

We have now established the clear and logical process that led to your situation in the first place. So we can draw some conclusions. The mind is capable. The logic is faultless in application. The "problem" must be with your "facts."

I hope by now it has become apparent that one single accepted but questionable fact is the shaky concept that judgement is necessary in the first place.

Eliminate judgement. There is no need to change either our actions or our beliefs, only the price we pay for them.

Judgement. The world is full of it (and you may translate that to suit yourself). The next time you have a conversation with one or more people, count the number of times you hear the word should. Possibly a therapist gets a distorted view of the language used by people in general, but it sometimes seems to me that the phrase "I should" is the single most used phrase in the English language. Interestingly, it's closely followed in popularity by "they should'" and "we should." When people are in a reflective mood, I hear "I should have," "We should have," "They should have."

It appalls me. It sometimes seems to me as though everyone is lurching down the street with this monstrous pile of "shoulds" on his back. I see people afraid to think in future terms or consider a cohesive plan of future action, simply because they are mired in a bog of options as to what they "should" do. Get people talking and you soon see their other pile, their "should haves." "I should have done this or that and things would surely have gone better." Self-judgement at its best.

Here we have bright, rational people, all busily telling themselves and as much of the rest of the world that will listen, how things would have worked out better. As the shoulds and should-nots, and the should-haves and should-not-haves pile up, their self-esteem is slowly, surely, and inevitable being eroded.

In an effort to avoid mistakes or errors in the future, these people are busy carefully reviewing their pasts, pinpointing their errors, while analyzing themselves and their actions to more clearly define what they "should have" done.

Now you and I have just established that you cannot

remember exactly what you were doing only five minutes ago. I suggest to you that it is reasonable to conclude that no one can remember everything exactly. So what do people gain from these ego-destroying exercises? One thing they obviously gain is a reason for standing still and not doing or trying anything different. They simply can't risk adding to their already monumental pile of "shoulds." They also reduce their self-esteem to such a low level that no one will throw rocks at them because they are too low to be seen.

But seriously, do you know what I have found to be their real gain in every case? Think about it yourself for a moment. What do you gain from leaving yourself open to all this judgement, both self-created and externally applied? (Remember that we established in Chapter 1 that you gain from everything that you do.) When you accept the judgement of others, you gain the "right" to judge them back. That's it. And we learn the process early in life. How old were you the first time you were called bad? I vividly recall a glorious cartoon in a local newspaper, where in every box, a little boy was called bad. In every frame it was "bad boy Joey" this and "bad boy Joey'" that and "bad boy Joey" the next thing. In the final frame a stranger comes to the door and asks "What's your name, little boy?". "Bad boy Joey" was the child's reply. It would have been hilarious if it hadn't been so tragic.

But then, what can a small child do? He has no way of fighting back because he doesn't set the rules. Quite often his first indication that he has broken a rule is when he does something for the first time. Also, it's a rare parent who will allow a child for long to respond with "bad mummy" or "bad daddy." So a child does the only thing possible to unload what has been put on him. It is bad brother, or sister, or mailman, or dog. At least he can diminish his pile by dumping on other people or things.

As the child develops sophistication, so his dumping process grows in complexity. Now he can get into right and wrong. He can get into should and shouldn't, ought and oughtn't. With further finesse comes more convoluted dumping.

"Joey should have gotten out of my way. Then I wouldn't have had to run him over with my bicycle." And as we grow older: "Of course I ran into the back of his car. But he shouldn't have stopped so quickly. Then I wouldn't have hit him." Now we are not only seeing how to get rid of judgement, we are able to pass the blame on too. With a little patience and a little practice, we can refine the process to such a science that we can avoid taking responsibility for anything that we do.

"I'm not overweight because I want to be. Oh no. My mother shouldn't have fed me all those things so I got a taste for them when I was small," or "My wife shouldn't bring the damn things into the house," and "The stores shouldn't display them so enticingly," and "They shouldn't allow radio commercials, television and newspaper ads," and "They really shouldn't show all that beautiful food that I shouldn't be eating. It's not fair. They're bad. I'm just a victim." If you buy that, there's a bridge I'd like to sell you in New York.

Sad, it is true, but on the other hand it is an inescapable fact that as soon as we get involved with even one other person, the judgements are going to start to flow from them. Get involved with two people, and you can multiply that by two, four people by four, and eight people by eight. Now begin to observe what is happening. Because I choose to live in a society with other people, it's important to me to know what they are thinking about me. That requires listening to their judgements as well as possibly flattering opinions. Most of us have a narrow range of good friends, probably some two dozen, and we commit ourselves to listen to at least one dozen carefully. To this we add a collection of up to a hundred others, made up from acquaintances, business associates, and other people whose opinions we can translate into success or failure in our chosen field and environment. I listen to those people too.

I want and choose to live in this society. By that act of choosing I accept the reality that this and all other societies have laws, morals, and standards, all judgements of which I had better be aware (note the judgement), or my chosen society will come down on me like a ton of bricks. So Instead, I come down on myself like two tons of bricks, just to be certain I haven't missed anything.

Each brick is a judgement. This isn't a pile of straw I'm carrying on my back, it's a brick house, and worse, it's three stories high. As my interests in the world around me expand, so too does my list of contributing judges, until it can encompass every other person on this earth.

Now we can begin to clearly see the deal that I have made for myself. When I insist on the right to judge others, I must (note the judgement), in all fairness allow everyone else in the world the right to judge me. I ask you, What in hell kind of deal is that? If I spend all day with a steam shovel, I can only dump back on about a hundred people a day, if for no other reason than that they are the only ones close enough.

What are my options? I can judge and be judged. Or I can give up judging and deny others the right to judge me. I can refuse to judge, and demand in return that I will not be judged. If as so often happens, in spite of this, some one or ones make a judgement, I can refuse to accept it. I can refuse to accept the judgement with all its ramifications, and hear it only as an opinion.

It is as simple as that.

Here is another part of the package. I accept without reservation the premise that I do only what I want to do. Because of this, I cannot blame others for what I do and what I am. It's a package. If I am willing to accept the responsibility for what I am and what I do, knowing that I only do what I want to do, the same applies to you. You do only what you want to do. You are what you want to be. I no longer need to take the responsibility for you or your actions. The same is true for all the other people in my world.

Here is the deal I make with everyone in my world. I accept the responsibility, but never the blame, for all that I do and all that I am, and I demand the same of you. Whether I accept or reject your standards, I will listen to your opinions. I will hear them as opinions, never judgements, simply because it is important to me to know what your standards are, what you believe, and what you value. All I ask in return is that you hear my opinions as opinions and not judgements, so you will better understand what can activate and motivate me.

The concept sounds simple. The concept is simple, but the application requires constant practice. The application is guaranteed to generate a rebirth in anyone who makes it work, but don't try to do it less than full out and completely. I assure you that using this concept in isolation can and will regenerate your life, but it is much more pleasant if you can convince those in your immediate environment that this is not only good for you, but good for them. To be convincing you need to be convinced. To be convinced, you need to practice.

Watching people become aware of the implications of this concept, especially in a group situation, is fascinating. I notice that their first reaction is always to sit or stand a little straighter as the weight comes off their shoulders, and they are braced by an increased awareness of self-worth.

Unfortunately, their next reaction is usually fear or concern that when or if they lay this on their friends, they will lose those friends. I can only suggest to you that if your friends desert you when you take this approach, you are not their friend, but merely their convenient dumping ground. I can't know about you, but I hope to be more to and for my friends. After all, this concept that is freeing me, is also freeing them. If this leads to rejection, we had better next examine rejection.

CHAPTER 5
REJECTION

In my experience, there are few things as destructive to one's self-image as rejection. In our society, few things seem as frightening as rejection. Look around you. Look at the billions of dollars spent every year on everything from face creams to cosmetic surgery, from perfumes to antiperspirants, and, yes, even how-to books like this one. Look at the fancy cars, opulent homes, sparkling jewellery, and plush furs. All are designed to show an outside world that we aren't rejected. We're accepted.

Rejection comes in many forms that we must avoid. There is the ultimate rejection: I don't want you. I don't need you. I don't like you. There is rejection by criticism: I preferred your hair/teeth/body odor/clothing/hat/religion/ideas before… There is the criticism and rejection by omission: You forgot my birthday/the garbage/the loaf of bread from the store. And so it goes on.

Let's try an experiment in rejection. For a few moments I would like you to pretend that you are a bright, healthy, acceptable, and deliciously feminine young woman by whatever standards you are using this week. It is your birthday. There is a knock at your door, and there I stand with this great big box. Adding a large smiling "happy birthday," I hand you the heavy box.

Sensing my excitement, you open the box immediately and find inside the absolutely finest football uniform that money can buy. The colors are your favorite colors, the numbers your lucky number. On the back, your name in your favorite letters. The shoulder pads and indeed all the pads have been custom-made to suit and fit you. The helmet has been injection moulded to fit your head and made from the finest materials to protect you from any eventuality. In short, it really is the finest football uniform that human cunning could conceive or money could buy, all tailored to suit and to please you.

Remember for the moment that you are a young lady. Are you really going to be thrilled with my gift? Even if your own fear of rejection is so great that you are incapable of rejecting anyone else, can you really accept my gift?

Be honest. Once you have gotten beyond the pleasant fact that I have remembered you and your birthday and have gone to more than a little trouble to demonstrate my high esteem for you, aside from the gesture itself, what is there of value for you, in my gift? Little, if anything.

Of course you won't be thrilled. Unless you are an extremely unusual young lady, you pure and simply will have no use for this uniform. Bluntly, you will reject it, if not out loud to spare my feelings, most certainly you will reject the uniform within yourself. And yet...

In total, the uniform is still the finest money can buy and ingenuity devise. Taken separately, the parts of this uniform are choice and tailored with you in mind. Still you reject it, and why? Because it is not of value to you. It is not of any use to you.

Can you see how something or someone can be of real, undeniable value, and yet not be of value to a specific someone else? The football uniform has undeniable value. It has intrinsic value. So do I. So do you. My needs and desires can no more change your intrinsic, real value, any more than your opinions can alter or reduce my intrinsic value. Our real value may increase or decrease, be more, or less important to any other person, but through it all, retains its constant intrinsic value.

The things we do and the things we believe also have a value, but again, their intrinsic values do not make them valuable to all people under all circumstances. I once spent a charming morning with a group of people at a Unitarian Sunday service. After a friendly ceremony, complete with delightful music, guaranteed to offend no one, the congregation gathered in a circle for tea and stimulating conversation. I understand that this is typical, and I found it most pleasant to get to know the individuals in depth through their discussions.

The accent of all the talk was on fellowship and kindness to fellow man through an awareness of his needs and wants. In general, everyone professed a high level of compassion for his fellow man. I was impressed with their sincerity and asked if this was the main thrust of their organization. I was assured that they wished to find and offer to everyone fellowship through kindness. When I pointed out that this simplistic approach would alienate a large portion of humanity, they seemed genuinely appalled. When I pointed out that this approach would surely risk alienating every masochist in the world, the meeting broke up.

For some reason, I have never been invited back. I wonder if I've been rejected?

I have had other problems with rejection. When my wife and I started courting, there was an evening when we were scheduled to go somewhere special; it doesn't really matter where. When I arrived to pick her up, it was obvious she was even more excited than the date warranted. As she twirled around for my gratification, I realized that she had invested in a new dress.

Now this may not seem like such a big deal to you, and it probably wouldn't be so thrilling for her today, but in those days, she was just recovering from being a starving music student. In those days, new dresses were few and far between. This dress was well cut, fitted her beautifully, and was obviously expensive by our standards at the time. It was in a lush plum color. I hate plum!

I am quite sure in my own mind that if the entire Folies Bergeres chorus line danced in front of me wearing nothing but plum head-dresses, I would be unimpressed. I don't even know my reason for such dislike of plum. But, to all you plum-lovers in this world I say exactly what I said, without apology, to my wife that night, I hate plum!

To say she was upset severely understates her reaction. I was quickly made aware that my dislike for plum was being taken as a dislike for her. My remark was a slight upon her tastes, and in passing, clear evidence of my own lack of taste. However, most disturbing to me was the realization that my remark had been taken as rejection, and not only of the dress, but of its owner.

Our relationship survived the trauma of that evening some thirty years ago. I have managed to maintain my self-respect for my honesty, as well as my irrational dislike for plum, by telling her this little story. If, the next time we meet, you are wearing an outfit of sky-blue and pink with purple polka-dots, and you ask my opinion, I can be mean and vicious and nasty, all under the guise of being honest. Or, I can tell you that I like it. If I am really out to butter you up, I can tell you that I love it, that it's you, and then watch your pleasure of the moment.

If I do a really good job of convincing you how much I really like it, assuming you wish to please me further, you'll probably rush out and invest in more of the same color combination. Just think of yourself with a dozen damn sky-blue and pink outfits, all overlaid with purple polka dots in varying sizes. You'll probably wear them at every opportunity when we are together. As the sight of purple polka-dotted sky-blue and pink becomes totally nauseating to me, you will begin to notice more and more often, that as you approach me, I have the look of someone about to throw up!

If I have said I like the outfits, and you know I like the color combination, how long will it be before you "realize" that it must be the sight of you that sickens me?

On the other hand, I will be stuck with the unhappy options of either seeing you dotted and pinked and blued and purpled, regardless of how I loathe the combination, or admitting to you that I lied in the first place. No relationship can survive lack of trust. Could you ever be expected to trust me completely again, if I were prepared to lie to you about the color of a dress? I doubt it, and recognizing this fact, I would probably foresee and predict the end of our relationship. Being human, I would probably choose to walk away first, to avoid admitting that I had lied, leaving you to wonder what you had done wrong to cause me to reject you by deserting you.

As I noted above, the story worked. Please don't misunderstand. I am not advocating that we all go rushing out to hit other people over the heads and egos with our honesty. That's neither productive, nor necessary. The two points to remember here are one, that the rejection of our clothes, the color of our cheeks, or even the color of our hair, need not be a rejection of the total package that is us. The crucial point is that whether I accept you, or anyone else accepts you, like the football uniform, you do have an undeniable intrinsic value.

If I reject the basic you, no problem. You can dress it up, paint and perfume it up, and parcel it so I will buy the pretty package. But you know and I know that perfumes wear off and packaging frays. Sooner or later we will get down to the basic you. How much more beneficial for us both, if you accept and recognize the immutable fact that, whether I accept you or reject you, what remains is what you are: Something of undeniable intrinsic value.

My prime recommendation to everyone in my personal environment is to live with and wear this sign at all times and for all to see.

"I am me. Something of value. Take it or leave it."

I am what I am, and having accepted this, I proceed to being proud of what I am. There is no other me. Therefore I must be the best me there is. To be sure, I can landscape myself so the surface me appeals to a broad range of people. I can be the chameleon capable of blending into any surrounding or environment. I can even get a perverse satisfaction out of watching people's shock when they finally see the real me, except for time.

Time is my only non-renewable resource. With only so much time to devote to my friends, I can only be of exceptional value to two or three at any given time in my life. I can't afford even to try to be all things to all people. I need all my energies to continue being me, and allowing you to be you.

When I try to be what you would like me to be, I must take some of my energies to test, cross-examine, and question what you want. This process would leave us little time to be ourselves, to find out what and who we are, rather than what others wish us to be. We would both end up as losers. We would both end up empty.

And so I ask again. When we meet my only request is simple. Look me in the eye and offer me this. "I am me, something of value. Take it or leave it." If what you are is something of value to me also, I will take you and gladly. If not, and without in the least way diminishing your intrinsic value, I will tell you up front and we can both go on to find others who are what we want and want what we are.

Before we leave that fascinating world of judgement/rejection, let's take a look at some of the other ways we have of arriving at a low opinion of ourselves, and some of the hard costs.

I have a watch. It is a good-looking calendar watch with a sweep second hand, 24 jewel Swiss movement, and leather strap, which was imported by a leading chain of Canadian jewellery stores. Bought before the days of battery-operated quartz movements, it does however have a self-winding capability and a good gold-filled case. I admit it isn't the world's most expensive watch, but it does have an obvious value above the norm. For twenty years I tried to sell this watch to people in my therapy group for five dollars. I was serious. The watch was really for sale, and only for five dollars. Yet in those twenty years, only one person offered to buy the watch, and she was so hesitant and concerned about the deal it wasn't finalized.

Now understand, I am not talking about trying to sell the watch to starving students who couldn't have come up with five dollars. Over the years my prospective customers have included many wealthy and astute people. Regardless, rich or poor, with or without watches of their own, the reaction was always the same. They were all suspicious and leery of the deal. Simply because I tried to sell the watch too cheaply, everyone was concerned. The lesson was equally simple. Whenever we try to sell anything of obvious value too cheaply, every potential customer wants to know the same thing. 'What's wrong with it?'

I showed them all that this was the watch that I usually wore myself. I showed them the maker's name and let them observe that it kept good time. I let them see that over the years the gold-filled case had hardly worn at all and even offered a money-back guarantee for a full week. Nothing could overcome their suspicions that because I was selling something too cheaply; there had to be some hidden catch, something wrong.

It doesn't take a genius to make the quantum leap to realization that if I can't sell a small machine with a few moving parts when I undervalue it, I can't possibly hope to sell myself if I undervalue or underprice myself. Neither can you.

It is most probable that you, like I, find people underselling themselves every day. Some call it modesty; some call it shyness; some even come right out and admit that they're not worth very much. Where do they get these low opinions of themselves? One sure way is by listening to and believing in the put-downs of others.

"Somebody is always putting me down."

"My friends - relatives - bosses - lovers - mothers - - fathers - teachers (you pick one) are always putting me down."

"They tell me I'm no good."

"I can't do anything right."

"I'm a mental or physical bumbler, or both."

Well hear this, you bumblers of the world. Every put-down is a compliment! I'll give you a hint and let you work through this one yourselves.

How often have you ever put down someone whom you perceive to be beneath you, equal to you, or whom you did not fear in some way? I suggest never. If I'm already equal or beneath you, and you have no reason to fear me, you don't need to put me down. It is only those you fear, or those above you whose levels you think yourself incapable of reaching who need to be put down. In fact, the process is really a pull-down; a pull-down to your level.

Think of put-downs, and in fact all judgements, as dirty balls, and recognize that you always have the option of dropping the ones that come your way. Even if you catch a dirty ball, nothing says you can't throw it back, but some of the muck just might stick to your fingers. Let the ball drop and that is the end of that game.

What immutable law says that a judgement is any different from a dirty baseball? I can throw judgements at you until I am tired of tongue and jaw. If you don't catch them, that's the end of that game too. When you think about it, the only difference between a thrown judgement and opinion is in the catching. As long as I'm selling and you're not buying, I'm throwing and you're not catching, I can't control you using guilt. Unless you choose to agree and become a catcher, the game called Control By Guilt is over before it starts. The same applies when you start to play catch with yourself. All the judgement phrases like should, and ought, and might have, are the dirty balls of the guilt game. Throw all your judgement phrases away permanently and avoid catching any more.

Have you ever gone through one of those sick-in-soul, sick-in-heart, sick-in-body, mind bending, and deep soul-destroying depressions? The ones where you just can't get the enthusiasm for anything, including living? The ones where sadness and sorrow just radiate out of you and nobody can miss it and nobody can fix it? Nobody, that is, except you. That's correct. That's what I said. You can fix it.

The next time you find yourself catching a depression, or even if you find yourself in the depths of one, look at yourself clearly and honestly answer the question "Am I really guilty?" In my experience, depression is nothing more, and let me add, nothing less than the result of judging yourself, finding yourself guilty, and punishing yourself with a depression. It answers all our needs as a punishment. Depression is self-controlled because it is self-inflicted. It is more than painful enough to convince us we have expiated our guilt, whatever that might be. Finally, it is obvious and as visible to others as if we, like the little boy, slapped our own wrists.

My only questions to you are, "Is it necessary?" and "Are you really guilty?" Review them yourself. If the circumstances indicate that you are not really guilty, unless you have also given yourself a cold, all symptoms of depression will amaze you by disappearing.

Here is another little concept for you to play with. Psychiatrists have long realized that the common cold and depression exist together and at the same time. The assumption has always been that the common cold causes depression. But let's consider the possibility that the reverse is true. I see it as entirely possible that people in the depths of a depression, particularly when they are not certain that they really are guilty, just might understandably have a need to cry. But, since crying would spoil the essential appearance of penitence, the tears must flow down the inside of the cheeks, the unspoken denials choke in the throat, and have to be coughed up.

It is an interesting concept, and when I have applied it to people who are in the process of catching a cold, and then convinced them that they are not guilty, their symptoms have cleared miraculously and within minutes.

COPING WITH EXPECTATIONS

We all cope with expectations. Our boss expects us to get up every weekday morning and show up prepared to work. Or our teachers expect us to show up for class.

Or our spouses expect us to work around the home if we don't go to work or school.

Society expects us to be law abiding. Western morality expects us to be monogamous. Our neighbours expect us to rake the leaves, and our local government expects us to put them at the curb in clear plastic bags. All pretty reasonable so far, but...

What happens if our mothers want us to become lawyers to fight for clean air, and our fathers expect us to become businessmen, even if that means polluting the air with industrial waste and fossil fuel residue? What happens if we favor our mothers and become lawyers fighting for clean air, but our job requires us to travel on polluting aircraft, driving polluting automobiles, working in offices and living in homes heated and run with the product of fossil burning fuels? What happens if our local government burns the leaves they and our neighbors demanded we rake and provide, only they add toxic fumes from burning plastic bags to the globally warming carbon dioxide? Suddenly, living up to the expectations of others ceases to be reasonable. In fact, it ceases to be plausible or possible.

One simple solution is to make all the expectations of others into our own expectations of ourselves. Now at least the problem is internalized and within our control, or is it? How long will it be before these internal conflicts impede our ability to function? How long will it be before the vast sea of expectations placed on us by others is simply too deep and suffocating to absorb? How long before the body rebels, even while the mind is still trying to cope? Something has to give before we create our own demise as the only reasonable solution to our dilemma.

In working with the short circuits that trouble our minds, one thing becomes quickly clear. Either expectations must go, or our ability to function will cease. Think about it. In a world with billions of people, broken into millions of pressure groups, communities, and nations, any single human being cannot even be aware of all the expectations placed upon him or her. Living up to them all is genuinely impossible.

Why would anyone try? The expectations of the boss who wants us to rise every morning and work are balanced by our own expectations of a paycheck, respect, and possible promotion. When our teachers expect us to show up for class, we meet this expectation with our own anticipation that we will learn, graduate, and benefit from the process. Spousal expectations are spelled out in marriage vows. When we agree to live up to someone else's expectations, we expect a beneficial return. It's a contract.

The process is all so logical, but it's based on a primary flaw. For every expectation of us, we have a corresponding return expectation of equal or greater value to us. But this is never possible in reality. For one thing, we simply do not have sufficient time or resources to even contact all those with expectations of us, never mind the skill or capability of forming a realistic contract.

When we make that basic contract with our boss or teacher, we agree to accept their expectations in return for them accepting our expectations of them. In reality, too often our expectations are ignored, denigrated, or simply not accepted. Resentment naturally flows when this situation becomes apparent, especially if the expectations placed upon us are left in place unchanged by a failure to reciprocate. Now those expectations become a burden instead of a contract. How many unfulfilled contracts are burdening you? How many of those burdens are accentuated by the additional burden of the uncontracted expectations of all those we cannot see or meet? Reasonable and logical as our original concept remains, in reality it cannot work, and does not work. To continue to try to make it work requires the acceptance of unreasonable burdens with their drain on our energies.

The goal in any consideration of our actions has to be benefit for ourselves. Others may benefit also, but unless our actions are dictated by a personal benefit, they are a burden. Whereas a personal benefit boosts personal energy levels and esteem, anything else is self-destructive. There is no such thing as altruism. Those who think there is, create an unrealistic life-model for themselves and a situation pre-conditioned to failure with its inherent loss of self-esteem and energy. If we add self-punishment for such failure, we see how the price becomes too high, and the gains too slight.

In group situations, we demonstrate the only way to cope with expectations. A soft ball or a pillow is named Expectation and tossed to the one having the problem. Usually the first time it is tossed, the victim catches the "expectation" and is often amazed when it is pointed out that they caught the expectation. On one of the succeeding tosses, finally the victim will deliberately not catch the expectation. This is the only way to deal with expectations.

Next the entire group throws a barrage of expectations. If the victim declines to catch any of them, they pile up around him or her, but they are not returned to the sender, not caught or absorbed by the victim, and not easily capable of being thrown again. This becomes a good time to recite the Gestalt Prayer, as enunciated by Dr. Fritz Perls, acknowledged father of Gestalt Therapy.

I do my thing and you do your thing.

I am not in this world to live up to your expectations, and you are not here to live up to mine.

You are you and I am I.

And if by chance we find each other, it's beautiful.
To which he later added,
If not, too bad.
Frederick S. Perls, PhD, MD.

If we accept the concept that we will abstain from catching any additional expectations, what do we do with all the old ones? When pressed, many victims actually feel the yoke of these burdens weighing them down. Palpable pressure handicaps them as surely as the weights a horse must carry in a handicap race. With the use of a little role-playing, we relieve them of this constant drain.

A facial tissue is place on a table in front of the victim. He or she reaches back, physically grasps hold of the burdens, and places them on the tissue. This role-playing is repeated until the victim can assure the group there is no sensation of weighted burden, and all of the burden is now on the tissue. Carefully folding the tissue, the entire burden is carried to the nearest toilet, and flushed away, with the parting comment, "Good-bye to all you expectations piled upon me by others and by myself!"

The victim is then encouraged to return to his or her place and sit quietly for a few moments, especially if as so often happens, the victim becomes quite light-headed.

It sounds so incredibly simple that even I am amazed at how well and how completely it works. When it doesn't, we have a window into the problem for the victim. Without exception, a victim who can't let go of externally applied expectations doesn't want to give up expectations they in turn have placed on others. These people are encouraged to try a few days without the sap on their energies caused by other's expectations and see if this is a beneficial deal for them. Give up being able to place expectations on others, for the freedom from the burden of other's expectations.

Expectations go by too many names to list here. People who would find it unthinkable to place expectations on you have no such problem with "hoping" you will do as they wish. Obviously you can't charge them with return expectations, if they are only hoping, or wishing, or thinking out loud, or wanting, or anticipating, or predicting, or trusting, or desiring, or contemplating, or any of the other euphemistic methods people use to disguise their expectations.

What does it all mean? Simple. When someone wants something from you, make a contract with him or her. Get it all out in the open and get something of value for yourself. No one else need know of your arrangement, and no one else can evaluate it, but if you deem it beneficial when you make the deal, only second-guessing can make the contract onerous and debilitating. Only you can later destroy the benefits of your deal with second-guessing, but that's a whole new situation.

I am me. Something of value. Take it or leave it.

CHAPTER 6
CONDIE'S
CONFOUNDING COROLLARY

If you have read this far, you should be feeling much better about yourself, right? If you buy that attempt by me to make you feel guilty, please re-read the previous chapters and review the concept of discarding "should" and other judgement phrases from your vocabulary.

Let's assume that you have received the message I have been trying to communicate. You have been able to recognize all the misconceptions, guilt-trips, put-downs, and other assorted judgements. We can now agree that you are not nearly as bad as you believed when you started this book. I don't believe assumptions are realistic under most circumstances, but let's face it. If I didn't presume that this book would have the desired effect on you, I would not have taken the trouble to write it in the first place.

So what happens if I've gone to all the trouble to write, and you've obliged by reading and understanding, but you still have this nagging doubt about your intrinsic value. You just know there is something wrong with you, and nothing so far has changed your mind. Here we have a blank wall. The kind of blank wall into which I, as a therapist, bounced all too often when confronted with an individual who just isn't that bad. We can often both see and agree that he or she is only misguided, misinformed, or pure and simply preyed upon by others to the advantage of those others.

I can work through and eliminate all the problems an individual perceives with himself and still be faced with someone who continues to maintain a low value of himself. Granted, not as low as before, but the anticipated lift of energy and spirit hasn't happened yet.

Consistent past results ensure my confidence in the Gestalt techniques that root through the conscious into the unconscious. I have confidence in my ability to know when individuals have trusted me with everything they can remember about themselves.

So, when my anticipated revitalization of an individual does not occur, I know there is something else. There was a time when I was inclined to believe that either we didn't have the whole picture, or my skills were insufficient to bring out the hidden, forgotten, or unrecognized important ramifications of something already reviewed.

A few years ago, a delightful young woman came to me for help. She was the baby of her family and had led a relatively sheltered life, growing up in a reasonably middle-class family in an upper middle-class environment. She was a study in contradictions. She was at the same time obviously emotionally unsure of herself and yet often poised. She professed to have a low opinion of herself, yet was dressed and groomed in a manner that belied this. She seemed and indeed was lonely and totally unaware of the attractive charm of her fresh appeal.

The young woman was a pleasure to work with. She displayed a bright intellect that quickly grasped and comprehended concepts over which others labored for many weeks. She professed and demonstrated an aggressive attitude in seeking progress and advancement in a business environment. Yet on the other hand there was the obvious though underlying hesitation in placing herself in any place of prominence or exposure. As we often see in these cases, there was also the standard difficulty we anticipate. There were problems maintaining and discomfort during close relationships.

Needless to say, her experiences were limited by her youth, but as we worked through them, we discovered the picture of a well-brought-up young lady, private to the point of being secretive, whose actions were all within the standards for behavior of a young woman in a modern society. By any current standards, she was a very nice girl. Nothing in her past seemed to justify a modest, never mind low, self-opinion. She was a sweet girl and a pleasant girl.

Despite this, and despite her apparent agreement that our assessment was valid, it became increasingly obvious that she was still being devastated by a self-doubt of her real intrinsic value, and our inability to find an answer was becoming a contributing factor. As usual, I attempted to dig deeper. Was there some forgotten incident? Nothing. We reviewed what we had already considered, in hope that some seemingly trivial incident had taken on unusual significance, possibly overweighed in importance because of her youth. Nothing. There simply was no circumstance in her life that could be seen to be damaging to her, or anyone else's self-esteem. There were two extremely traumatic experiences in her young life that did keep coming up again and again during our search, but there was no question of our young woman being to blame for either. However, they did keep coming up.

As a very young girl, I gather somewhere in her early teens, she had been raped by a stranger who attacked her in the street. She could not remember being threatened, but sadly she had been unable to confide in anyone about the incident, and so it remained a festering sore.

The second trauma came as she just happened to arrive home in time to see her pet cat run over and killed, dying in some considerable agony.

Either of these situations could be expected to leave traumatic scars on an impressionable young girl, particularly one who was essentially both sensitive and loving. This I could see. What I could not for the life of me see, was how being an innocent victim could lead anyone to conditions of lessened self-image and esteem. Slowly but irrefutably, we came to the answer together. It seemed so simple. It seemed so simple after we had the answer, that it is still hard for me to understand how it had not been seen before.

As a child in a typical middle-class environment, with typical middle-class values, she had been taught that if she were good, something good would happen to her. She was also taught that if she were bad, something bad would happen to her. I firmly believe that the concept of "good" and "bad," as taught to our children, can be improved by exchanging "acceptable" for "good" and "unacceptable" for "bad," and by taking the time to explain both in clear detail. On the other hand, I am well aware that the concept of

55

good and bad has been passed onto and, yes, often thrust upon parents when they were children, so I cannot fault them for accepting what they often could not decline to accept.

Unfortunately, in this and other instances that consistently confounded me, the people involved have applied the lessons as taught and sadly gone on to formulate their own tragic corollary. What they end up with is a four-pronged attack on their self-esteem.

1.)   If I am good, something good will happen to me.
2.)   If I am bad, something bad will happen to me.

To these are added:

3.)   If something good happens to me, it must mean that I have been good.
4.)   If something bad happens to me, it must mean that I have been bad.

I must have been bad, therefore, I am bad!

No one can fault the logic behind the conclusion. The basic error is in the original premise. The reality is overwhelming. No one, parent or otherwise, can guarantee a child that a life of being good will result in a lifetime of good things happening. Conversely, there simply aren't enough police in this world to ensure that for every bad thing that is done, something bad will happen. Even at this point in the equation, most children recognize that the parental premise is not always correct. When a child is good, we all know that something good does not always follow, and when the child attempts to complete the situation by making something good happen, he is all too often told that this is bad.

When something bad is done, and the promised retribution is not forthcoming, the child is faced with the necessity of making something bad happen to complete the situation. Again, surprise, surprise, all too often this is viewed as something good by the parents. The phrase, "You've made your bed, now lie in it" comes to mind as one choice selection from the parental phrase book.

When children and others compound the miserable inequity of the first two misconceptions with the tragedy of the second two corollaries, we have a confounding situation guaranteed to be a therapist's nightmare. It is also an assured tragedy for the unhappy individual who has stumbled into this unhappy connection.

What can anyone do who has fallen into this trap? Review the concept and the logic behind it. Can you accept it? Can you accept it for yourself or for anyone else? I hope not. Once you are certain that you do not accept either the original concept or the possible corollaries, and that they are no longer valid for you, discard them. Throw them as far from you as you possibly can. Waste no time on recriminations upon yourself, or those who taught you.

Take a close look at your history as you remember it. Have you fallen into this trap? Has your self-esteem been diminished because you "must" have been bad, and now you recognize that you weren't after all? Update your thinking. You can't remember exactly what you were thinking five minutes ago, so don't try. What is real and what is here and now is how you think and feel about yourself, here and now. Accept the reality of this new insight. Like the young lady who brought me to this understanding, you may more reasonably be considered the victim. You just may be someone of value after all. Accept it. Enjoy it. Like the young lady, allow your spirits to rise now you are freed from old weights and old horrors.

When you have had time to savor the sensation, we can go on from here.

CHAPTER 7
UNDERSTANDING PEOPLE

To understand others, it is of immeasurable assistance to comprehend ourselves. It also requires forsaking several deeply ingrained personal beliefs.

We cannot assume that conversing with someone in the same language will lead to mutual comprehension. Flatly stated, we may believe that we speak the same language, but actually, we rarely do. Another pet belief about to fall is that as individuals we are totally unique. On the contrary, we humans are extremely similar. I propose that for the moment at least, you trade your beliefs for mine, which will be more useful to your understanding of other people.

When you understand yourself and understand your own motivation, you will know others and also what motivates them. To genuinely understand others, we all too often have to choose between listening with a built-in need to establish facts or listening to hear the message others are attempting to convey. There are no relevant facts in human relationships, only perception. Humans act and react according to what they perceive, not facts, though they may call them facts.

Words mean different things to different people. Even people brought up in the same community, with similar educations, similar religions, and similar ethnic backgrounds all perceive word values differently. Words have often the simplest of differing shades of meaning, which we can establish from definitions in any well-researched dictionary. Add to these defined shadings, those that derive from local usage, and we begin to see the multiple permutations and combinations available in word values that have convinced me that we seldom speak the same language.

Others before me have clearly formulated the science of semantics. I propose to develop and hone in you the art of comprehending. Early in our marriage, I discovered myself in the midst of an extremely heated argument with my wife over what I believed to be a relatively simple aberration in our mutual standard of behavior. I found the variance mildly irritating and had previously requested either a change in approach, or at least a warning to me that it was going to happen again. Now isn't that a nicer way of putting it than just saying I can't remember what the damn fight was all about?

What I do remember was my amazement when I found a situation, on which we had reached agreement during an earlier discussion, had changed nothing. Not only did it not lead to altered behavior, but it was now leading to a highly emotionally charge argument that left me baffled.

I was all the more baffled because the point in question was so relatively minor that my main purpose in mentioning it was to inform my new wife that her actions were causing me minor irritation. I had expressed my irritation, thus getting rid of it for me. I sincerely believed that changing her actions would be simple and relatively undisturbing for her. I had left the first discussion believing we had reached an agreement that she would make the simple change. How could such an uncomplicated situation evolve into an argument so emotionally charge that it seemed to threaten our marriage? The elementary explanation is, we do not speak the same language. In this case, we had a totally different understanding of a single word. We each had our own interpretation of the meaning of the word understanding. My wife and I have extremely similar backgrounds. We are nearly the same age. We both have Scottish ancestry. We were both educated primarily in or near the city of Toronto, with similar religious backgrounds, modest middle-class homes, and at different times, both studied music with Eric Rollinson and psychology with Fritz Perls. It took a long night to realize that we didn't speak the same language and to begin to comprehend why.

My wife's mother was apparently often ill, often disturbed, and often seemingly irrational. Afterwards, when she explained her actions to my wife, who seemed to take the brunt of the irrationality, the mother would not justify her actions. She would merely ask my wife to understand. This my wife clearly recognized as a request to both comprehend, and either condone or forgive her mother's behavior. Unfortunately, my wife quickly came to realize

60

that understanding usually led her to being the loser. She had to end up either forgiving the unforgivable, doing without while others did not, or being alone in accepting the short end of the stick in some other way.

Being a logical human being, the only way she had to balance the loss that understanding constantly caused her, was to seek reciprocal gain by demanding understanding from others, including from me. Over the years, she had met sufficient other people with a similar misconception of the meaning of the word understanding, to make her system work.

When I presented her with my original minor complaint about my irritation with her behavior, she quite contritely apologized for irritating me and explained the reason for her actions. She requested that I accept her reasons and realized that she had not intended to disturb me in any way. At the time I could appreciate her logic and the pattern behind her behavior and so admitted. It was at this point that she requested my understanding, and as I was later to be reminded, she was most insistent that I did understand.

I did understand. I did not *understand*. "Understand" to me means comprehend, period. When I told my wife that I understood, I was simply telling her that I comprehended what contributed to her actions. What she heard was that I both comprehended and condoned her actions and that, in understanding her, I was also forgiving her. No way!

When the big day arrived and it became obvious to my wife that I had neither forgiven nor condoned her actions, when she knew that I had, the minor disagreement exploded. It became entirely insignificant compared to my betrayal of her trust with my inability, or worse, unwillingness to keep my word and understand. We had been painfully careful to build our relationship on honesty and trust. My lack of understanding was shattering and led directly to the emotional intensity of her reaction.

It took a long night and a fortuitous trip to the dictionary to begin to resolve the depth of a problem created by our differing interpretations of one single word. In addition, you can imagine my shock when I realized that, to my wife, I appeared to forgive her. I don't believe in judgement. Without judgement, my forgiveness is meaningless and utterly without value to her or anyone else.

I still find it difficult to remember that despite our similar backgrounds and similar environments, we can't totally trust our communications to our mutual language. Over the years, by being more explicit with our choice of words and watching each other to learn what we mean, we have established a workable common language, but it was months before we could say hello at breakfast without a handy dictionary.

How equally difficult it must continue to be for those couples who first meet, then try to communicate. How potentially destructive to their self-esteem when they seemingly fail to express their most basic natural reactions, yearnings, and needs. I was fortunate and learned from experience that in understanding people, the message is more important than the facts.

A number of years ago, I bought what I took to be a little round footstool. Seems fairly straight forward doesn't it? I asked for a footstool. The salesman sold me a footstool. Here we have an item that stands approximately fourteen inches above the floor, on four turned legs with leveling devices on the end of each. The top is flat bottomed and the top is slightly curved, padded, and covered in a green fabric. It is a footstool, right?

How wrong. Over the years, people have placed drinks and food, books and papers, and a multitude of other things on this handy table. It functions well as a TV tray. Using a magazine on top, it works well as a writing desk. Turned upside-down by children, it's been a turtle on its back, a somewhat greenish chariot, a sled, a throne, and an armchair. It has been a stepstool for fixing ceiling tile and curtains, and a podium from which countless important orations have issued. It's been a steering wheel for everything from an automobile to buses to monumental ships, and yes, even a 747 jet. Here is a genuine flying-saucer come to land with its green color giving full credence to the Martian theory.

So who is right? Is it a stepstool? Or is it a Martian landing ship? I could go through all the many variations of what this item might be, could be, or is, but the important fact remains simply this. When discussing this item with someone, it is more important to know what each individual believes it to be, rather than know what is right.

In human communications, there is no right or wrong if communication is our genuine intent. Of course, I always have the option of boosting my own ego by demonstrating that I know this object is a footstool, or whatever. I can insist that others recognize and accept my definition. My alternative is to risk really getting the message people wish to convey. I can try to see what they believe or want to believe, regardless of whether I agree or not.

Make no mistake. There is a real risk in communicating. I risk getting your message. I risk the possible need to change what I believe. When I like and accept myself, this risk is minimal. When I do not accept myself, this risk can be uncomfortably threatening for even the slightest change to my thinking or believing patterns. There is also a risk when I try to give you a message. We have already seen how we may not speak the same language. We have seen how a simple object may not be the same thing to both of us. If you are of value to me and I find that I can't communicate with you, how shattering this is for my self-image: how disturbing to our relationship and how easy it is to blame myself for these failures.

Here comes the judge again.

Here comes guilt.

Here comes sentencing and with it the inevitable punishment, either self-injuring, or self-deprecating with its loss of personal regard and value. Be fair. Does this demand a sentence of guilty? We have seen how we probably don't speak the same language, or have a common recognition of common objects. In this case, communications problems do not warrant negative judgement and loss of esteem.

Am I at risk from possible other failures in my attempts to communicate? Yes. But again, the problem does not realistically reflect on any individual. Trigger words and trigger phrases are something we see every day, and yet we cannot realistically anticipate them, nor can we anticipate the strength of the reactions they precipitate. There is not even a way we can forecast the direction of someone's response to his or her own triggers.

If, in the context of casual conversation I say the word dog, and you have four friendly, happy, supportive, and loving dogs at home, you will respond with warmth. Just the mention of the word dog can open a floodgate of warm thoughts, memories, and reminiscences. The excess may form a warmth that spills over me without my quite knowing why. On the other hand, if three of your animals had to be put down this morning, possibly after being poisoned by the next-door neighbor you thought was a friend, what a different reaction I can anticipate, after the fact, of course.

Man or woman, you may burst into tears of either sadness or possibly frustrated rage. Weak or strong your breakdown into sadness may overwhelm your previously maintained good front of social obligation. If you loved your animals, your entire reaction could swiftly change from an internal sadness to a radiant anger that projects over and through me. Only if you explain in detail, possibly more than you may wish to express at this time, will I have any hope of comprehending the strength of your reaction, and recognizing that though seemingly directed at me, it is not your intent to be angry with me. Only with your complete explanation can I come to know that the problem was simply in my use of the trigger word dog, and not some failure on my part to communicate. In any event, I will need to cling to all my resolves of earlier chapters to avoid feeling guilty for having hurt you.

Some time ago, I walked in on a conversation between my wife and one of her older pupils. I immediately sensed a very heavy sadness in the room. They were talking about one of our favorite neighborhood squirrels, which had somehow lost his fine bushy tail this year. He now looks like a small rabbit until he climbs a tree. I immediately realized that the pupil was obviously saddened by the thought of our poor little squirrel that had lost his tail. I didn't need to be a genius to understand that. Here was a circumstance much in need of humor to lighten the sad situation, so I told them both the story of the rabbit that lost his tail crossing the railroad track at the same time a train was on the track. When he turned around to retrieve his tail, the next wheel took off his head. The moral of course being that one should never lose one's head over a piece of tail.

While I agree this is not the absolute funniest of tales, at least it was apropos, and in the past evoked considerable happy response. Not this time. This time the story fell flat with a thud, and gloom returned like doom to the room. The sensation was so strong, I had to leave, all the time wondering what on earth was going on that I didn't comprehend. What I later learned in a scathing rebuke from my wife was another sad story. The pupil in question had just returned home from two week's holidays in the south, only to find that during her absence her pet rabbit had taken sick and died. The animal had been put to sleep without her having the opportunity to even say goodbye.

Here indeed was the classic case of a trigger word or phrase, and the dilemma it creates for anyone who pulls that trigger. I certainly couldn't fault my awareness, since it gave me the perception to sense the sadness in the air. I couldn't fault my intention, which was to lighten a heavy conversation. Since this was an old joke, told many time over the years, I would not even consider faulting my delivery. Past laughter was sufficient to provide statistical proof that the story was normally funny and well told. No, the main fault was that I failed to achieve what I intended. There was also a failure in my audience when they did not live up to my expectations, with their sad reaction to my story. (Please review the previous section on expectations.) Here was a situation full of failure, full of negative reactions and responses, and overflowing with opportunities for guilt.

How many times have you inadvertently pulled a wrong trigger? Take a minute and think about it. You call a new lover "sweetheart," only to find that his or her last relationship, which was a totally disastrous emotional time, was spiced with "sweetheart" even when breaking up. The last words were "get lost, sweetheart," or something to that effect. Needless to say, the response to your "sweetheart" is negative at best.

You cheerfully advise your boss to "have a nice day," only to find that when his wife bought herself a new mink coat, the bank canceled his overdraft and called his note. Try to get a positive response to your nice-day jazz under those circumstances. Have you ever noticed how being in a happy mood can be upsetting to someone because they are in a sad mood and want to stay that way?

How can you win? You're right. There is no end of possibilities for making disastrous communications with the best of intentions. Similarly, there is no end to the possible permutations and combinations of potential self-judgement, self-conviction, and self-punishment. Inherent in all these situations is the potential for further reduction of self-esteem and loss of self-worth.

We have just gone through some obviously extreme examples of possible negative reactions engendered by equally obvious trigger words and trigger phrases. But these examples presuppose an honest and open reaction from people with whom you are dealing and a visible reaction. What about those who are only mildly triggered, or those whose reactions are more tightly controlled? How can anyone really know how often in a given day or given circumstance, our conversation, however well intended, is in reality evoking negative responses? When these are directed at us, how can we know that these reactions have nothing to do with us directly? How can we know that these are not reactions to us or what we are, but only to the trigger words or phrases we have inadvertently used? How can we avoid using them and causing the hurt they bring?

There is no way! A Siamese twin who has lived side-by-side with a twin, might have sufficient knowledge and awareness to know all the situations that might have created trigger conditions. For anyone else wishing to avoid triggers, you simply don't have enough information to hold any hope. Even if we do grow up together, because my reaction to similar circumstances will be dissimilar to yours, at best all you can do is guess what might be a trigger and guess at what depth or intensity to expect from my response.

If you choose, in spite of the obvious impossibility of avoiding these situations, to indulge in the game of guilt, be forewarned that you cannot win. As you look deeper into this problem, it is to be hoped that you will recognize this as a microcosm of all your relations with all other people. You cannot win the game of guilt. Our only hope for winning the game of life is to totally discard the entire concept of judgement, guilt, punishment. If you contemplate continuing on religious grounds, note that even the Bible instructs us to "judge not, lest ye be judged."

There is no reasonable way that you can be aware of what may or may not upset me, or for that matter, turn me on. Short of ceasing to communicate altogether, there is no way you can even hope to avoid the triggers and all the other things that might distress me. Even if you keep quiet, if I have been ignored too often in the past, your very silence can be a trigger. You can't win using these rules. You can't even break even.

There is one way I have found to get us both off this vicious merry-go-round. Change the rules by which we live and play. "I do not expect you to take the responsibility or the blame for my reaction to you or your actions." "I categorically refuse to accept the responsibility or blame for any response you make or reaction you have to me or my actions." "I take full responsibility for what I am and what I do, and for my intent, but none for your response."

How do I know you are being honest? Because I also categorically refuse to be responsible for living up to your expectations of me or life, I do not expect you to live up to mine.

CHAPTER 8
HURT FEELINGS

Have you ever seen a trout attack a fly on a calm pond? The fly flutters down through glistening sunlight and settles on the surface of the shimmering water like a feather. Suddenly there's a streak of silver flashing in the light almost quicker than the eye can follow, and zip, the fly is gone and swallowed. The scene is graceful nature at its best.

Unfortunately for the trout, the fly is often laid upon his shimmering plate by a crafty angler. As our swift and graceful diner heads home with its expectedly tasty fly, it is suddenly jerked up short, painfully stabbed, and now totally in the control of something outside itself. The fight may be on, but the trout has been hooked.

The closest parallel I can draw in the human condition is the reaction I see in some people hooked by the simple phrase, "You hurt my feelings." When cast by an expert, it hangs on the breeze just like the fly. When the unsuspecting victim swallows it, anyone can watch the similarities with our unhappy trout. Instantly the individual is stopped short in his or her tracks. You can practically feel the painful barb bite home. Just as certainly as with our friend the trout, struggle as our victim will, once the hook is accepted, we are able to watch control pass to some outside agency: The person/angler who cast the phrase.

Fritz Perls said many times, "Show me someone whose feelings you are afraid to hurt, and I'll show you someone you perceive to be spiteful and vindictive." Let's face it. If someone were not spiteful and vindictive, we would really gain little by avoiding hurting his feelings. I believe that most of us can agree that hurting someone's feelings usually brings some disadvantage for us. But have you ever investigated how one goes about hurting another's feelings? What feelings are we hurting? Think about the last time someone hurt your feelings. Let's go one step further and consider what feelings are.

With each new therapy group, one of the first exercises we work through will always be on feelings. Each group member is asked to give us five feelings, prefacing each with the phrase "Here and now I feel. . . ." The exercise has two specific intentions. One, to bring everyone's focus into the here and now rather than the past or the future. As we have previously demonstrated, we can't remember the past all that clearly, and the future, though sometimes anticipatable in some respects, is always an unknown. In coming to grips with understanding the individuals in a group, it is important to become aware of what is going through his or her mind, now and in this place, because this is the only reality with which we can make contact.

The second intention is to clarify a definition of feelings as a lead into other insights. With most groups, numbering between eight and fourteen people, almost without exception, I can anticipate hearing all of the following feelings.

❑ Apprehension
❑ Concern
❑ Curiosity
❑ Fear
❑ Excitement
❑ Stress

These recur more often in new groups, or with those people in a psychotherapy situation for the first time.

After going around the complete group and collecting each person's feelings, we go over the group again, asking those who have stated any of the above six feelings to describe exactly where they feel these feelings. Regardless of how valiant the attempt to localize and describe the above, it quickly becomes evident that these feelings are in fact not feelings at all. They are *thinkings*. Without question each individual does feel something. He may feel pressure in his chest where he believed he felt concern, fear, excitement, etc. We quite often find evidence of reaction to apprehension or excitement in the bowels or bladder, but the feeling is pressure or tension, not apprehension or excitement. It is a typical reaction of a person under mental stress, developing a physical reaction to his own thought processes. With this insight, we instantly lose a whole list of *feelings* from our vocabulary, and replace then with thinkings.

In the process of getting to the roots of many of our people's problems, we encounter another group of feelings called emotions. The list will usually contain one or two of:

- ❏ Hate
- ❏ Anger
- ❏ Love
- ❏ Desire
- ❏ Resentment
- ❏ Feeling attacked
- ❏ Feeling supported

Again a request from the therapist to describe and localize actual feelings of love, hate, etc. points up the reality that actual feelings are warmth, tension, and so on, and are often the result of, and reaction to the individual's perception of hate, anger, resentment, and other intellectual emotions.

What does it all mean? What does it all matter? What could anyone gain from differentiating between thinkings and emotions or feelings? Think about it for a moment. What do you gain from calling apprehension a feeling and resentment an emotion? I believe it all goes back to our upbringing, which tells most of us that we can and must be held responsible for what we think, and some groups even want to judge us accountable for our thoughts. Our feelings and emotions, on the other hand, supposedly come to us unbidden and un-called-for. There is an implied expectation that others will recognize that we cannot be held accountable for our emotions and feelings, only what we do with or about them. They can't be controlled, they being simply a natural response to some outside stimuli. Who could possibly be responsible for his feelings? Can you now see the advantages in misinterpreting thinkings for feelings?

71

How effective do you believe our control of another human being would be if we hit them right between the eyes with a stern, "You hurt my thinkings"? Not too much I expect.

But what is in it for us if we take responsibility for our own thinkings. We could demand those in our environment recognize the difference between thinkings and feelings, and take responsibility for their thinkings, as we accept responsibility for ours. Imagine it. No more hurt feelings to hook us. No more outside control by others. All because we are willing to be responsible completely, but only for ourselves.

Convince those around you that you offer opinions, not judgements. Accept responsibility for what you are, how you are, and why you are what you are. Then demand in return that others do the same or leave you out of the game.

Accept responsibility always. Never accept blame. It's a nice way to live.

CHAPTER 9
UNLOAD YOUR HEAVY PAST

Unaided by therapy techniques, we have seen how unretentive the memory can be for the normal and usual events of living. However, under specific sets of circumstances, the mind seems to fill the memory, and these recollections can be tapped or triggered.

Can you look back in your experience, at least five years, and recall a particular incident where someone hurt you? It can be a physical, mental, or so-called emotional injury where you were the victim. If you can remember such a situation, please think about it in a little more detail. For instance, can you see clearly in your mind the person who injured you? Here and now, can you actually recreate the entire circumstance in sufficient detail to genuinely sense the same responses you were having at the time? The hurt? The upset? The painful down feeling? As you feel the impact of memory, can you feel again the same stress within as you felt at the original injury, and at the original time? In my experience, I can look back on many such situations, where members from a group have created not only a recollection but a memory of the intensity of their reaction to the situation. These memories can be revived as much as thirty years after the incident. Note I said the memory was revived. The memory and the facts may or may not be exactly the same. In comprehending what motivates people, it is less important to know the facts than to know what they believe to be the facts. You are not influenced by the facts of a situation, only your remembrance of them.

Working in therapy groups, I have seen people stimulate themselves to actual tears over such long-lost situations. We've all watched the fight going on inside someone as they recreate both predicament and response, especially if that response had little to do with the original hurt. Why is this memory so clear and others less clear? The key is in the usually unexpressed response. At times when clear-cut responses would have been noticed and of some value to the situation, we often and for our own reasons do little to express ourselves.

Present me with this sort of situation where something has happened to you that demanded a response you did not make (even though it was for reasons you found valid at the time), and with your help I can recreate it years later. I can approximate the actual intensity you felt during the time of the problem. Not surprisingly, Fritz Perls called this the unfinished situation, or the incomplete Gestalt.

We only do what we want to do. This includes standing still.

Someone slaps our face prompting a natural reaction to slap back. When we don't, we always have our own reason for holding back.

"They're bigger than I am."

"If I hit back I could start a fight I cannot win."

"I've been brought up to turn the other cheek." (Makes sense when you think about it. Turning the other cheek gives much better balance for counter-punching.) Unfortunately, we often only turn the other cheek and repress our natural animalistic nature. Note! I said repress, not control.

Whatever our reasons for not responding as our reactions dictate at such a moment, once we are aware that there is no altruism, we can be sure of one thing. We must have had a valid reason that was logical to us at that time, and in that place. That being the case, next comes the obvious question. "Why is memory still so sharply clear and fresh to me today?" Here again we find a concept more readily defined than applied. Practical use and practice are required to gain maximum benefits.

When something happens to me that prompts a reaction that I then stifle or repress, regardless of the soundness of my reasons at the time, I will have created an unfinished situation. The memory of this incomplete Gestalt will remain with me in strength and detail till expressed or till it dies with me. To be more explicit, the details as I remember them will remain. Fritz Perls loved to tell the story of memory and ego always arguing. Memory said it was thus, but ego said no, it was thus instead. Ego always won! Except to comprehend our own memory process, to us it does not matter. We are motivated by situations as we see them in our own context, and by remembering, the memory becomes a fact of and unto itself. This is our situation.

There are two ways to complete an old unfinished situation. I can go back to the situation if it still exists and completely express all that I repressed, or I can forgive. It doesn't matter if the situation was something outside of myself or of my own making. I can express myself, or I can forgive. That's right! Believe it or not, we can forgive even ourselves, but as I warned earlier, it takes practice.

On first consideration, expressing myself always seems to offer the most satisfying alternative. Reflection however brings realization. I perceive a benefit in everything I do. There was a benefit perceived by me when I indulged in repression in the first place, or I wouldn't have repressed myself. If I have difficulty remembering my original reason(s), it is most likely that here and now I will continue to repress rather than challenge the unknown, and just in case my original reasons are still valid. These could come back to haunt or hurt me.

Another consideration would be a situation where I know I am carrying something around with me, but I can't put a finger on the exact circumstances. All I have left is either an uneasy feeling that there is some old weight on my back, or inconsistency in my patterns that tells me something is there. All I know for sure is that I am still carrying it around with me, and I am still using the energy required to hang on to it.

That's what I said. I am the one who is using the energy to hang on. How much of your energy is being drained by the effort to carry old situations from your past, into your here and now? Are you hoping to become strong enough, or wise enough, or independent enough to risk the expression of those things you had in mind in the first place? Open sores in the mind and heavy weights on the soul! These are an awful price to pay for the off chance that you might express yourself in the future, maybe, if you think of it.

Want another way?

Try this instead. Take a large tissue and place it on a table in front of you. Now you get your chance to really be an actor. Try this even if you believe it to be unduly melodramatic or even foolish. The results are worth the effort. Physically reach back with your hands and pick up every little seed of discontent from your past that has been riding on your shoulders. Remove them to the tissue in front of you. Place them carefully. These are your long preserved memories. Keep picking and placing until you can genuinely feel that all the weight has been taken from your back, and preserved on the tissue.

Next, reach up to your head, and, in one handful, grasp all the unhappy things you have been remembering about people, places, and things, and place them on your tissue. If one sheet won't hold them all, get as many as the job requires. Keep picking and pulling, until you can really feel that the weight is gone from your back and the strain from your head. When your head feels light and clear, you've probably got at least the most of them on the table in front of you.

Look at the pile in front of you, and examine it in detail for the last time. Cry if you wish. That is your millstone you're looking at on the table. Talk to the pile. "I don't need you any more. I'm going to risk making room for your replacements. I don't want you any more. I don't want to drag you around with me any more. I'd even rather forgive you for the unforgivable, and get rid of you." Let it all hang out until your chest feels lighter too.

Now comes the hard part. Take the corners of each tissue, and carefully fold them over your pile. Turn each into a ball that you can carry carefully, or crush as you go directly to the nearest toilet and flush the whole mess away with a simple "Goodbye." Watch as they disappear from your needs forever. They're gone. You're free.

Now return to your table and sit down for a few moments until your body becomes adjusted to what will seem at first to be a weightless condition. This is what living can be like. No dead issues to drag you down. No dead weights adding restrictive burdens like a racehorse with a handicap. All that's left is the here and now with its warm anticipation of a future without the drag of yesterday. No more unfinished situations. No more incomplete Gestalts. Live it up. You're free again. You're just you again. You can live and like it again.

CHAPTER 10
TAKING OUT THE
GARBAGE ISN'T LOVE

Now that we've gotten rid of your old millstones, let's see if we can set up a screen to sift out future millstones before they can replace the ones you just flushed away.

Bear with me while I seem to belabor the obvious. If someone walks up to you in the street, asks your name, and, after you have carefully and clearly identified yourself, calmly belts you between the eyes with a two-by-four, I think we can both agree he's trying to hurt you. I believe we would both agree this is a deliberate attempt to injure you that would warrant and justify your responding in a somewhat negative manner. Because it is an obvious attack, your response is equally obviously justifiable. Because it is both obvious and justifiable, there is little doubt you will react in person or in concert with others and attempt to complete the situation and the Gestalt. Unless some major irreparable damage has been done by the original attack, this type of situation usually becomes complete quite quickly. This obviously direct and deliberate attack is not the type of occurrence that usually leads to repression and unfinished situations.

When someone comes up to me, identifies me, and proceeds to lash out with his tongue, berating, accusing, and generally attempting to injure me verbally, this attack is also obvious. Here too the justification for my response is as obvious as yours was to your two-by-four. Because of this, I too will most likely respond, granted in kind, and complete the situation. Because I can be certain the response is justified, I can respond without concern. Simple, and it is rarely a problem.

Now let's review the sort of event that occurs where the intent of the doer is not so obvious. I am walking down the street past a construction site, when some unseen body overhead tips a two-by-four from a third floor scaffold. When I hear the noise and look up, it smacks me right between the eyes. When I compare the lump on my head with the one you got from your malicious attacker, I can find little meaningful difference. The size is the same. The area of colorful contusion is the same. In discussing the situation with you, our heads seem to hurt equally. But. Am I justified in attacking in response to this accident, even though our injuries are equivalent?

In our earlier example of a tongue-lashing, let's assume that my attacker said flat out, "You're an S.O.B." Compare this with an overheard conversation from a woman who states after her third cocktail at a party, that all men are chauvinistic pigs or worse. Later she adds, "All males are S.O.B.s." I am male. If I was that close, she should have known that I could and would hear, so I can reasonably conclude that she has called me an S.O.B. Or can I? Can I equally justify attacking her in response to her broad statement that seemed to include me? I am a fair man. I realize that things are often said after a few drinks at a cocktail party for effect, not intent. But how do I determine her intent in this case?

The two-by-four off the scaffold, activated by someone unseen by me and therefore unable to see me, and the ambiguously directed statement have two things in common. I cannot as easily justify, to myself or others, attacking in response to these injuring, but accidental attacks. The second common feature is that if I choose not to respond to these perceived attacks because I am uncertain whether these can be taken as justifiable attacks on me, I will create an unfinished situation. These are the kind of cute ones that can stay with me for the rest of my days. It's a "catch 22" situation, isn't it? I can be damned if I do and damned if I don't.

The moment that I start to believe that I must justify my actions or reactions to anyone, for whatever reason, I leave myself wide open for the unfinished situation syndrome. If there is a chance that in reviewing the circumstances in preparation for finding justifications, I let the time for response slip by, I'm hooked. As soon as what I consider a reasonable time for response has passed, so has my best opportunity to get rid of the potential weight from my back. I risk carrying another incomplete Gestalt to my grave. Again, there has to be a better way, and there is.

To my wife I say, "If I don't take out the garbage, that oversight does not signify that I have stopped loving you, at least

80

not in itself. Conversely, taking out the garbage does not offer my best proof that I do love you." To the friend on the street whom I snub as I rush on my way to the hospital to have a fourteen-inch gash in my arm sewn, I say, "Dear friend. This is not a real snub as it seems to you. I just thought that chatting pleasantly with you as I bled to death, wouldn't be much fun, long range, for either of us."

My actions are predicated by my needs. For this I do not apologize. Your actions are predicated by your needs, as you perceive them, and I neither demand nor expect an apology from you. This is not some self-centered view. This is a fact that I hope we established to your satisfaction in Chapter 2.

If I choose for my reasons to interpret your individually motivated actions as an attack on me, simply because they do not suit my needs, I am the one who is being unrealistic. If I compound the gall by attempting to accuse you of attacking me or my self-value, can you really hold yourself responsible? Of course not, I hope.

If you burp at my dinner party, is that an attack on me? Are you really doing something to or at me? Even if I had asked you in advance to avoid what we both know is a problem for you, when you slip are you attacking me? Am I being realistic considering this an attack on me, or simply trying to control you by guilt?

Look at the whole picture. I want to accept the responsibility for my actions and for myself. Period. In fairness, I offer you the same prerogative. There are doubtless going to be a myriad of inadvertent and also direct actions of yours, which will not always meet and fill my ideal desires. We can compound your potential problem if we choose, by showing you that the same action by you, under different circumstances and at other times, can be misconstrued at will. I am equally certain that my actions will not always meet your ideal specifications for you.

So here are my options. I can choose to take all your actions, direct and indirect, relate them to myself and my needs, and find fault when your actions or lack of actions don't meet my standards. I can then consider that you have injured me. In fairness, I will be obliged to offer you the same choice in return.

These injuries which we sometimes choose to perceive from others, when they are really only doing their own thing, make for beautiful unfinished situations. If the injuries come from someone who is close to us, or of value to us, their self-serving actions, if taken as an attack on us, can lead to our undervaluing ourselves. The more we value the other person, the greater can be our own devaluation. It's a mug's game! If you've been playing it, do us all a favor and stop. More important, root out the old injuries that you have been carrying about like some festering sore, and see if in the light of this new insight they could be disposed of, or simply left behind.

We can choose to believe people honestly fulfill their own needs with no malice intended for us, deliberately or inadvertently, or we can choose to allow their simple self-serving actions to erode our self-value. The result leaves us feeling ignored, unappreciated, and unvalued. I have never sought nor hoped for sainthood. I am certain some of my actions will sometimes distress others. When I get a job, someone else does not. When I eat a pear, someone else does not. When I earn recognition, someone else does not. However, those people do us both a disservice when they attribute these actions as somehow an attack directed at them. They are not. As always, the choice is ours.

CHAPTER 11
CONCLUSIONS

What does it all boil down to in the end? To what have you exposed yourself with your effort to read this far? I believe in the Gestalt Prayer, which says I'm not here to live up to your expectations, and you're not here to live up to mine. I won't try to tell you what you should have learned. I am going to encapsulate the methods and concepts I have been trying to convey, to offer the same ideas in a slightly different way, to help to make them yours, in your way, for you. I know that as long as they are my ideas, they won't be totally successful for you. Think of them as seeds, offer them a chance to grow and become yours: to click for you. Then and only then will they work completely for you.

The concepts I have outlined in this book have been tried by many people from many differing segments of population, with many differing degrees of intelligence. People's intellectual capacities do vary. That's not a judgement, that's awareness. I am also aware that if my concepts had not touched you in some way, or created some glimmer of recognition in you, there is no way you would have reached this point in the book. Unless of course, you are simply checking to see if the butler did it . . . . too. Therefore, and again this is not a judgement, complimentary or otherwise, there is no doubt in my mind that you are above average bright.

Thus, you suffer from the two-edged sword. You have the intellect to build emotional problems for yourself, the capability of working your way through them, and with luck, the savvy to avoid judging yourself for going through a potentially needless process in the first place. I have tried to show you that everything you do benefits you, just as others act to their own perceived benefit. The more social an animal you are, the more you will perceive among your benefits, socially acceptable behavior.

I have tried to show you that all human acts follow a logical, for them, pattern once we know the complete story. I have tried to show you that when we understand ourselves, we have all the tools necessary to understand everyone. You are no better or no worse an animal than I am. Regardless of whether we agree on that statement yet, I hope that at least you have now reduced better and worse to the status of opinions and not judgements. I can also hope that all the shoulds and shouldn'ts, oughts and oughtn'ts, rights and wrongs and all like brothers, have been disappearing from your vocabulary.

I am also hopeful that by now you will have revamped your opinion of yourself, recognized your own intrinsic value, and you will now have a sufficiently high opinion of yourself that we can begin to build a relationship. Want more proof that there is no such thing as altruism? You thought I was writing this book for you. I'm not! I'm writing it for me because I'm sick and tired of meeting people whom I like, and with whom I could enjoy spending my time, only to find that their woefully low self-value, based on unrealistic appraisals, dooms our friendship before it can really start. We may never meet dear reader, but if we do, I'll be ready, and I will have done what I could to help you to be ready to form a genuinely meaningful relationship.

Did that last statement pique your interest or reactivate your guilt syndromes? Have I convinced you with my concepts of guilt and punishment based on the double-standard judgements that we all absorb from our upbringing? Have I convinced you to take responsibility for you and only you? If so, I'm succeeding. Have I at least got a defense attorney in your perpetual mental courtroom? If so, again I'm succeeding.

Have I convinced you to take only the responsibility for your intent, regardless of how you or others eventually view the results?

I'm reminded of the story of the combined church picnic and young people's golf tournament. Picture if you will a bright green and grassy starting tee of a shiny new golf course, clustered with a host of healthy young people waiting to start their game. At every vantage point around the tee, stand the obvious workers of the church, resplendent in their robes and uniforms of office.

The afternoon proceeds with both dispatch and commendable decorum until one young man has the sad misfortune to swing and completely miss the ball. "Oh damn!" The words ring out across the gathered multitude creating a crashing silence over all. Shaken by his awareness of the impact made with his chosen phrase, but undeterred, the young man proceeds to take an even more monstrous swipe at the offending ball. If possible, the swing misses the ball even more ignominiously. Knowing where he is, but unfortunately not having read Chapter 2, the young man allows his brimming frustration to burst forth in an even more vehemently uttered, "*Oh damn!!!*"

The words reverberate around and through the quiet crowd now shocked to petrifaction. Then the assembled ranks part like the Red Sea before Moses, and out rushes a sweet little nun. Storming away from the crowd, she plants herself indignantly before the young man. "Do you know what will happen if you say that even once more?"

"No."

"This clear blue sky, which now reaches all four horizons, will suddenly cloud up from north and south, from east and west. These clouds will rise to gather into a rolling boil directly over your head. From this black mass a fearful flash of lightning will blaze to swiftly strike you dead, here on the very spot where you stand." With this, the nun marches to the edge of the tee leaving a slightly stunned young man alone with his ball.

Collecting himself with all his courage, the young man makes a more determined wave at the ball, which, impelled by his mighty thrust, trickles ingloriously some three inches from its original spot. He raises his club prepared to slam it to the ground, remembers where he is when he notices the elders of the church all watching, checks the still clear sky, and resigns himself to being mortal. He slams the club into the ground and with a scream more cry than call, "*Oh DAMN!!!!*"

Everyone watches in fascinated horror as the little nun rushes to her place before the young man. Looking up, she summons dark clouds from every horizon. They race to a thunderous meeting above the young man's head. The promised jagged bolt streaks down from the darkened heavens . . . . striking the little nun stone dead.

The silence is total, only to be slowly penetrated by a growing rumble from the heavens that erupts into a fearful roar from above,

"Oh DAMN!!!!!"

What can I say? It happens to the best and the worst of us. What we start out to do with unquestionable merit of intentions becomes distorted with some fickle wind or circumstance. Often, we can even achieve what we intend, only to find the recipient of our efforts now wants the opposite. Learn to live with your intentions and let the results please whom they may. This is the concept of taking the responsibility for your intentions, not some other's perception of the results.

Recognize that you have an undeniable intrinsic value.

Recognize that being honest is being kindest, if not short-term, always long-term, and so much easier to live with.

Never sell yourself short. Few people want to believe their friends can be bought cheaply, for if nothing else, this undervalues both friends and friendship.

See your depressions for what they are: Your depressions: The price you seem prepared to pay for thinking (note I said thinking) guilty. It is convincing, but is it necessary?

If I have succeeded, you can now be aware that communicating can be a risky business. Let the whole world see that you take the responsibility for what you think, what you feel, and what you are. You accept responsibility for you, but only you. All you ask of the rest of the people in this world is that they do the same.

Get hold of a friend or relative, or anyone reasonably at hand and try this little experiment. Reach out with your right hand and grasp the other person's right hand, turning your palm upward so that the back of the other hand is level, and facing upward. Next, place a small weighted object on the upper hand. Now easily and simply demonstrate to each other how easily and simply you can jointly lift the little weight. Next, lower your hands to the original position, but this time both of you pull away from each other as hard as you can. Now try to lift the little weight. Much more difficult to lift anything when you are being pulled in opposite directions. Physically, intellectually, and emotionally, when part of you wants to go one way and part of you wants to go the other way, the simplest of processes become monumentally difficult.

In this book I have tried to show some of the ways and the patterns of some of the ways in which people fight themselves. They find themselves guilty in a courtroom without defense counsel. Bad things have happened to them, so failing to find accurate justification or acceptable explanation, they come most unjustifiably to believe that they must be bad. Between such self-inflicted wounds, those presented us by others seeking control, and a continual war going on inside us, it is truly incredible that we can function at all!

I hope I have succeeded in some way to help you unload the vast debilitating, vaguely remembered piles of past experience, past judgements, and past everything with which you struggle while trying to survive in the here and now. That is my hope, not some expectation being laid on you at the last minute.

When and if we meet, I also hope my intellect and sensitivities will be sufficiently clear for me to see you as you are, here and now. With any luck at all, you too will come to our meeting unencumbered by the past. I will present you with my firm belief. "I am me. Something of value. Take it or leave it."

Regardless of which you do, I make you this promise. I will walk away from the meeting secure in the knowledge that I am something of value . . . and so are you.

The End

ADDENDUM A

The test that forms the main part of Chapter 3 is one that I have used for many years. Given verbally and in person, it has been consistently effective. However, to ensure that the written version that you find here would be equally effective, the written test was given to a collection of people who were not involved in the Gestalt Group. These people were friends, friends or acquaintances of friends, all of whom took the test without prior coaching, just as you find it in the book. I requested blind responses, so there is no need to protect identities, but as a group, the candidates all appeared to function well but were hoping for improvement in their living skills. It works.

Lists have been arranged so match ups are aligned, at least relatively so, but nothing has been changed or left out. I will add a few comments after each list, giving you some of my interpretation of why certain items have been matched, while other connections and asterisks have been left to you to think through and draw conclusions. In reality, without asking the individual personally, neither you nor I can guess for certain what was in someone else's mind, but the projections we make can provide us with an interesting insight into our own thinking.

Over the years I have found, with few exceptions, that all items cancel out in one way or another. The item could be equally valid on either plus or minus list. We find the same item on both sides of the list, or we notice blatant contradictions regardless of which side we find them. This exposes the prime value in this exercise as a visual demonstration of how monumentally dependent we are on judgements when we assess ourselves.

On one of the demonstration lists you will notice sensitive vs. oversensitive and serious vs. too serious. Judgement is so clearly emphasized when a positive characteristic is turned into a negative by the quantitative judgements "over-" and "too." For me, these are the types of judgements this exercise highlights till they just jump off the page to get my attention. It is like a repeating nightmare as judgement after judgement completes its self-destructive abuse of the self-judging individual.

Read through these examples and the commentary. Learn how to spot both the obvious and the disguised match ups. Use your own intuition to develop a sense of what monkeys each of these people have on their backs. Then return to your own list. Root out the unnoticed judgements and establish a non-judgemental assessment of what and who you are. Let your list tell you where your anchor swings, then take a fresh and realistic look at what you have to offer.

Consider this. If you offer the world an individual who is positively sincere, and someone for their own advantage takes too little or too much of that sincerity for them, it's like cooking with salt. If it doesn't work out to someone's satisfaction, is the problem with the salt, the soup, the cook, or possibly even the diner?

NOTES ON TEST LIST #1

Sensitive is shown as minus. Could this not equally be a plus depending on the pleasant or not so pleasant nature of the stimulus? Trusting is shown as a plus, but if someone had just taken advantage of our trust, it could just as possibly have been a minus. The same logic applies to most of this list, but some of the others give us room for conjecture. Morbid is a hybrid of fearful and somewhat of a contradiction of trusting. It can be a result of perfectionism, in that the owner of this list doesn't wish to die either imperfect, or before he has had a chance to reach his perfect self-image. This could be a self-generating cycle if he can convince himself that he won't die until he reaches perfection, and so assures himself of everlasting life by the simple expedient of never allowing himself to reach his vision of perfection. This can be accomplished by setting unrealistic goals, or disrupting his endeavors with things like fear or impatience.

Is it safe to guess that he was most bullied when he declined to give?

Impatience and enthusiasm could be the same thing viewed from my perspective of whether he was doing it my way, or contrary to my way.

Unless someone is critical of us, alone is not a human characteristic, but rather a condition, usually brought on when the people in our current environment decline to reciprocate the traits we find valuable in ourselves.

Spoiled and giving are flat contradictions and would seem to indicate two judgements coming from different sources.

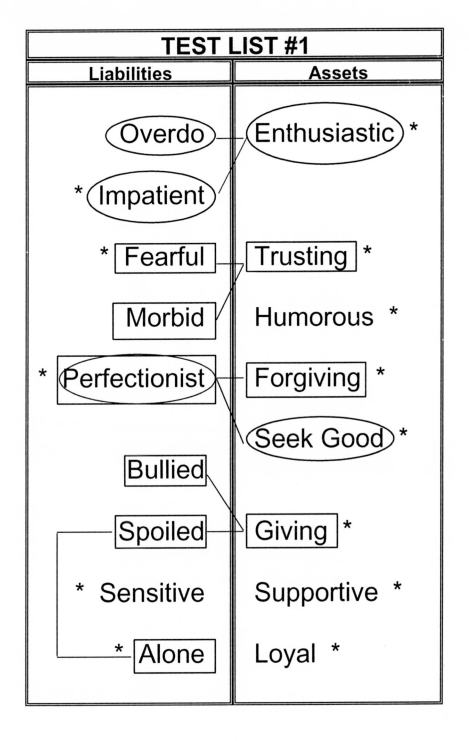

NOTES ON TEST LIST 2

Here we have someone who claims to be unsociable, but on the other hand has a small group of close friends. Here also, someone who believes himself to be a poor conversationalist, yet shows that prime attribute for conversation, the facility to be a good listener.

We have someone who sees or has been taught the virtue of modesty, but lists being unconfident and unassertive as liabilities.

A generous person only becomes a spendthrift when her generosity to others or self exceeds her means or budget. Can a person really be generous if her generosity is contained well within her budget? Or is it more likely she is generous to one who gains from her, and a spendthrift to those she denies?

A generous person who is a good friend to a small group of friends has reason to hope that those friends can be depended upon. When personal exclusivity is repaid only lightly, it could be considered reasonable to be angrily disappointed. Could this be jealousy?

Here again we have someone who sets high standards. I sense another perfectionist. Are these possibly double standards? Could the setting of high standards and being unrealistically perfectionist, lead someone to become lazy, just to avoid the predetermined failure? We can see how becoming a modest failure, i.e., unsuccessful and untalented, might lead to a lack of self confidence, being unassertive, unsociable, dependent, and yes, even jealous of those not so hung up.

All of the above, with only the possible single justification of preserving the image of someone who might out-succeed or out-achieve friends who might leave rather than try to keep up?

Is it worth it?

TEST LIST #2

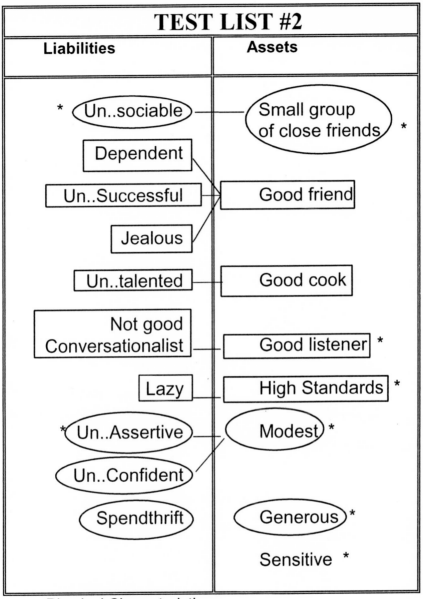

Liabilities	Assets
* Un..sociable	Small group of close friends *
Dependent	
Un..Successful	Good friend
Jealous	
Un..talented	Good cook
Not good Conversationalist	Good listener *
Lazy	High Standards *
* Un..Assertive	Modest *
Un..Confident	
Spendthrift	Generous *
	Sensitive *

Physical Characteristics:
- ❏ Underweight
- ❏ Crooked nose
- ❏ Big Ears
- ❏ Overbite

NOTES ON TEST LIST #3

Can anyone explain to me how someone who perceives himself to be flexible, sensitive, generous, giving, understanding, and a nice person, could possibly consider himself unlovable?

Is it possible that this nice person is like Fritz Perls' good little girls, behind all of which he always found a spiteful bitch? As he explained it, being a good little girl meant doing what others designated as being good because those others wanted such conduct. With so many of those others wanting so many differing standards and requirements, and making demands to accommodate their preferences, it is no wonder someone might resent such persistent but inconsistent direction. Resentment quickly turns to spite.

This whole list suggests someone who is being bombarded by, subjected to, and sadly catching judgements from all directions.

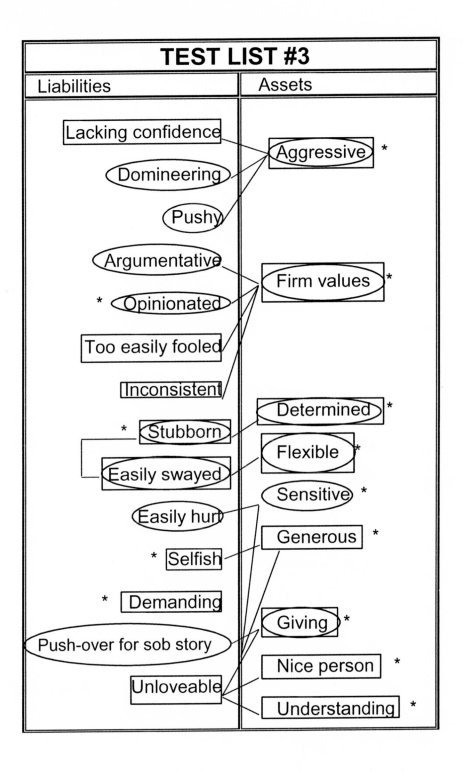

TEST LIST #3

Liabilities	Assets
Lacking confidence	Aggressive *
Domineering	
Pushy	
Argumentative	Firm values *
* Opinionated	
Too easily fooled	
Inconsistent	
	Determined *
* Stubborn	
Easily swayed	Flexible *
	Sensitive *
Easily hurt	
* Selfish	Generous *
* Demanding	
	Giving *
Push-over for sob story	
	Nice person *
Unloveable	
	Understanding *

NOTES ON TEST LIST #4

Here we see the classic example of the mental conversion of assets into liabilities through the application of quantitative and qualitative judgements. We see "over-" and "too," the "in's" and the "un's."

What we are left with is a person who is oversensitive, too serious, indecisive, and unsure, but by whose standards? This person is honest by his own admission. The judgements must come from someone else.

What could a sensitive, imaginative, and dreamy individual become except paranoid under such dishonest evaluation? I, too, would turn to art and music.

TEST LIST #4

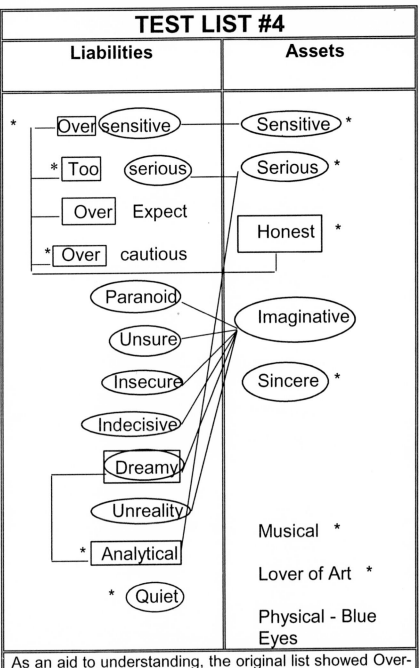

Liabilities	Assets
* — Over sensitive	Sensitive *
* Too serious	Serious *
Over Expect	Honest *
* Over cautious	
Paranoid	Imaginative
Unsure	
Insecure	Sincere *
Indecisive	
Dreamy	
Unreality	Musical *
* Analytical	Lover of Art *
* Quiet	Physical - Blue Eyes

As an aid to understanding, the original list showed Over-expect as "Expect too much from people," and unreality was "often hard to face and deal with realities."

NOTES ON TEST LIST # 5

Talk about your study in contradictions. You would think with a pole this long in either direction, the result would be a burdened but at least well-balanced individual. And we do see some hope.

When he finally realizes that regardless of who originally proposed his contradictions, he is the one carrying them around today, all by himself, recovery is on the way.

When he starts seeing opinions instead of criticisms, constructive or otherwise, there is no doubt that most, if not all of his liabilities will become supportive assets instead of debilitating drawbacks.

Either way, looking carefully at what this person has to offer, could you ask for more in a companion? Could you ask much more of yourself?

*****

TEST LIST #5

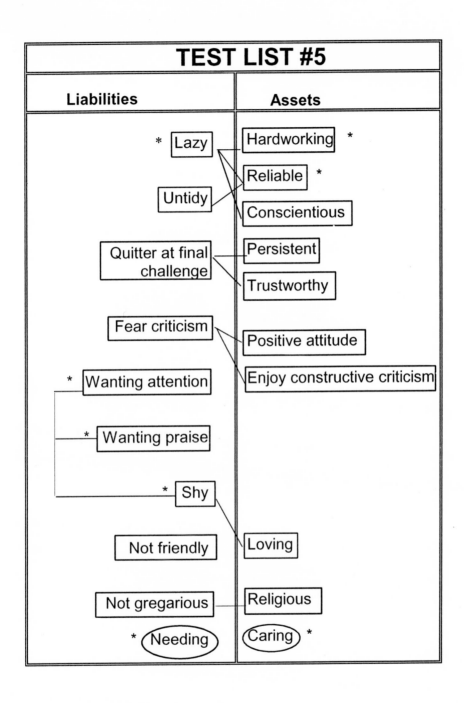

Liabilities	Assets
* Lazy	Hardworking *
Untidy	Reliable *
	Conscientious
Quitter at final challenge	Persistent
	Trustworthy
Fear criticism	Positive attitude
* Wanting attention	Enjoy constructive criticism
* Wanting praise	
* Shy	
Not friendly	Loving
Not gregarious	Religious
* Needing	Caring *

ADDENDUM B
ON CURING AND AVOIDING THE
COMMON COLD

Over many years, people, particularly the British, have attempted to establish a causal relationship between external conditions and the common cold. I have personally talked with students who took part in experiments that included going to sleep outside in beds with wet sheets. To the best of my knowledge, no direct link has been established.

On the other hand, there have been psychological studies that consistently linked depression with the common cold. The studies concluded that people got depressed, which caused colds. In my twenty-five years as a psychotherapist, just the opposite is true. First comes the external conflict, then a repressed response, then the cold. The depression is often a result of internal spin-doctoring, which concludes that since I am miserable, I must be guilty of something. I may only be guilty of going out without my galoshes, or hat, or scarf. The most difficult to cure are those who haven't actually done anything "wrong" but "know" they must have.

I contend that, given cooperation, I can cure, i.e. eliminate the symptoms, of any cold if I get to the sufferer within the first few hours of onset. The methodology is simple. I contend that within every one of us are sufficient strains of cold virus to keep us sniffling and coughing permanently. I am sure you have seen such patients. However, within us all is also the variety of antibodies needed to keep the whole mess in balance, and thus control. The virus only gets the upper hand when we allow a psychological stress to upset that fine balance. For the common cold, there are two such stresses that lead to symptoms. First is a desire to cry, repressed, leading to the Pagliacci Syndrome, crying on the inside while laughing on the outside. The tears flow down the inside of the cheeks instead of the outside, thus the running nose. Second is a desire to say something, repressed, leading to the "cough it up" syndrome, and the victim's cold starts with a dry cough. I have not been able to check with every culture and language, but over the years I have discussed this with a surprisingly large cross-section. In every language and culture there is an equivalent for the crying on the inside, and coughing up something unsaid. Have you ever noticed how asking a child what is wrong when he coughs, usually quiets the cough while he is telling you? It only returns when you stop listening.

Once under way, the unrestrained virus can affect all parts of the body. However, by eliminating the need/repression conflict at onset, almost magically, the "cold" disappears.

There is a risk with some strong-willed people as I have found with my wife Daryl. Many years ago I was able to convince her that her cold was brought on by a need to cry about a particular situation which she could not change. I was able to define the situation and get her agreement that the cause had been identified. The cold disappeared, but apparently I was unsuccessful in relieving the conflict. The next thing I knew, she had a bladder problem that took both medicine and deep discussion to clear.

How to resolve the conflict: crying/not crying conflicts usually have some basis in oft forgotten dictums by those hurting us, to either be brave, be grown up, or be stoic about life situations. This conflicts with a natural tendency to cry when physically hurt, distressed, or faced with sad situations. In working with patients already emotionally disturbed or distraught, I have found the most repetitive hurt to be hurt feelings. By demonstrating with the individual that hurt "feelings" are actually hurt "thinkings," I give control of the situation back to the individual. If the only "hurt" is that created by response to some outside situation, the "crying" reaction can be eliminated. The cold disappears.

For other crying situations, getting the patient to either cry on the outside for a short time, or helping them reassess the situation to the point where they no longer have the need to cry, again resolves the conflict, and again the cold disappears. A typical example of a repression situation is tears of frustration. A simple example is where the butcher promises a Christmas turkey of sixteen pounds, and the day before Christmas delivers one 18 lbs: too large for the microwave. It is upsetting. It can be frustrating if you are into that sort of reacting. It also can usually be resolved since it is the day before, not the day of Christmas. The stages usually are:

1) Anger at the mistake being made, repressed because you don't want to upset a good butcher, or because you have been trained never to get angry etc.
2) Frustration at not getting what you ordered, and not being able to express your reaction.
3) Tears at not being able to express the building frustration, possibly already at a stage of accumulation from other unexpressed reactions.
4) The belief that a turkey is not worth crying over completes the conflict, and sets up the internal stress to which I believe anti-bodies respond, leaving the cold virus unchecked.
5) The entire situation then becomes" depressing" as second-guessing begins.

This is a theory to be sure, but my success in curing depression with an absolutely simplistic method, indicates a sound basis in probability. I simply require people to ask themselves this question. "Am I really guilty?" Answers usually start with "Of what?" to which I reply any number of potential second guesses such as "Should I have used another butcher?" "Am I guilty for trusting the one I did use?" "Should I have written it down for him, complete with the explanation that my microwave only holds up to a sixteen-pound bird?" (Note how often the words should, could, and ought appear in the answers.) By this point the individual is usually adding to the list of possible personal errors, usually all unrealistic. Once the individual accepts that he or she is not guilty, the depression disappears, and with it many of the cold symptoms if caught early.

Coughs are usually even simpler to cure if caught immediately while the incident is still fresh in the individual's mind. Find the repressed conversation, and get the patient to either express what has been repressed, or re-evaluate the need for expression as a function of personal advantage. As example: The boss makes an unreasonable demand. The reaction is to tell him off. Repressed, this can lead to a coughing cold. However, expressed to the boss this can lead to firing. With recognition that the individual's overall personal best interest is served by being silent, the control of the situation reverts to that individual, repression is eliminated, and so is the cough.

Sounds simple, is simple and effective. By being aware of myself and eliminating internal dichotomies, I have personally eliminated the common cold for the past thirty-four years.

Regardless of how seemingly, even personally destructive my behavior is, I am convinced that everything I do has my own best interest at it basis. There is no such thing as altruism. I can't always bring to mind the exact benefit I find in all my actions. However, over the years I have traced the patterns in myself and others often enough to be totally convinced. My teacher, Dr. Fritz Perls, was of the same opinion based on an even more extensive survey.

From this simple theory follows the best method for "curing" what is often considered aberrant behavior. I ask the patient what he gains by non-productive actions or attitudes. Sometimes the actual active gain is achieved by not doing something. Then I ask him to compare the situation that originally prompted such self-beneficial actions with his present situation. This is done by comparing himself and his actions against the changing background of his environment (the basic Gestalt, i.e., Gestalt Therapy figure/background relationship).

As example: a large man is afraid of small dogs. Compare conditions when the fear was first noted, i.e., when the man was small and the dog was relatively large. Point out the change and you change the perceived self-beneficial pattern. Fear of dogs is eliminated to the exception of actual danger from attack-trained dogs, or ones exceptionally large and vicious.

The concepts are amazingly simple, and only implementing them becomes complex. A therapist who remembers that even the most extensive variations all respond in time to the simple concepts can usually produce remarkable results, even "curing" the common cold.

ADDENDUM C
BASIC PATTERN FOR USE IN
THE ANALYSIS OF DREAMS

AS DICTATED BY DR. FRITZ PERLS TO ADVANCED THERAPIST MEETING

Mechanics:

1) Relate or write down the dream as recalled.

2) Repeat above, observing any unrelated aspects. Use these unrelated aspects to find any points missed.

3) Make note of all associations, memories, and feelings connected with the dream. Express any opinions and interpretations.

4) Dramatize the dream. That is, act it out as it happened. (Note on times:
   a) Be sure to use the present tense at all times;
   b) Be sure to place all props, people etc. in their proper place relative to the subject.)

5) Make an inventory of all people, objects, structures, moods, emotions, and relationships.

6) Act out identification by form, each and every item of the inventory until the symbolic value or essence of each is understood.
   (Note: this is important. If there is a chair in the dream, the subject must become that chair, or cliff, or river as the case may be.)

   a.) Act Relate each item as well as the total dream to the subject's "life dream," i.e., his subconscious desires and aspirations for a life as it would ideally be for him. Note that this does not mean to relate to a life dream that is given lip service for publication, but to the sum total of the subject's aspirations, both conscious and subconscious.

Understanding the method:

It is most important to understand that this method does not attempt or have any use for dream analysis as commonly practiced in standard dream books etc. Whether a cow for example is consistently symbolic of any specific event etc. is a subject that I do not intend to argue. Suffice it to say my experience has shown no evidence to substantiate such claims. In fact, evidence consistently refutes all such claims.

This is an analysis of the subject, and only the subject. It is an analysis in the present, of a subject in the present, and will show the subject's mental attitude as it is in the present, not to-morrow; not yesterday. It is important to realize before starting analysis that:

1) This is not a painless process. If deep-felt emotion were not brought up in the course of the study, the value and depth of such analysis would be subject to question.

2) Definite and strong resistance will be encountered from the subject; i.e., there will be hesitation to use the exact word as it first comes to mind when describing a feeling or emotion. Repeated statements such as "I feel foolish doing this." "What possible good can come of my acting as if I am a river?" and "It's impossible to act out being a large space of air between a wall and a fence." This is a normal reaction and it is important for the analyst to remain persistent and outwardly unmoved by such resistance.

3) It is necessary to stress feelings and emotions in the acting.

SAY GOODBYE TO GUILT

Emotionless recitations of physical characteristics of a chair, river, etc. will only prolong analysis.

4) **Most important!** The more impossible it is to act out the feelings of a normally inanimate object, the more the subject will project his own true subconscious feelings into the act. It is these descriptive adjectives of emotions and feelings that I strive to reach. The more spontaneous their use, the more I can depend on them to reflect the real subconscious mind of the subject. As the inventory list dwindles, a pattern should establish itself, or a series of patterns of adjectives describing a similar type of emotions will repeat themselves, and adjectives describing opposite emotions normally appear, i.e., fear, worry, anxiety, and conflict, vs. courage, calm, relaxation, and peace. This is what I am looking for. This is what must be related to the life dream, and the subject, with a little encouragement, can usually admit to the state of mind revealed by his acting.

ADDENDUM D
ON BEING SATISFIED

One big secret to living comfortably is to be satisfied with what you have, and yet continue striving to improve your circumstances where you can. It is the difference between moving forward from a secure footing and foundation of satisfaction, and struggling to improve from the unstable underpinning of a second-guessed past.

When you accept the reality that you only do what you want to do, who you are, what you are, and where you are in life are all the result of choices you made with your own benefit in mind. Second-guessing is a treacherously easy trap into which those not honest with themselves often fall. Dissatisfaction is usually a result of second-guessing or completely ignoring the package principal. Few if any of life's decisions are straightforward choices between one of two simple alternatives. Usually you are offered a choice of two packages made of benefits and drawbacks. The formula for living satisfied with your present state is to remember that you bought each segment as part of a package and to always review that decision as a package.

How often have you heard someone say something like:

"I really love my car, but I wish it had a different grill."

"I really like my boyfriend, but I wish he were

a.) taller

b.) shorter

c.) quieter

d.) noisier

e.) less aggressive

f.) more aggressive."

"I like my car magazine, but I wish it had more articles on rock collecting."

"Going to school is okay, but I don't like having to do homework."

"Ice skating is fun except for the cold."

"I wish I had a smaller nose, bigger feet, and nicer body."

Let's take a look at these unsatisfactory situations, and see if we can discover a common cause for dissatisfaction. When someone owns a car, it is most likely that person bought or accepted the car as a gift. The choice was his. Now he denigrates the package he originally approved. The seats are still fine. The engine is still fine. The steering is still fine. The price he paid is still fine. Only the grill is unacceptable. Now when he drives in his car with the fine steering, engine, and seats, he is unhappy, not only with the offending grill, but with the package that is his car.

The moral of this story is that once you buy a package, it is illogical to pass judgement on anything less than that whole package. Our car owner is not miserable with the package he bought. Only the grill has become a problem, only the grill that was on the car when he bought the original package. Does it make sense to enjoy your car, but be dissatisfied with the grill? When you buy a Chevy, you get a Chevy grill. Honda owners expect to get Honda grills. A Chevy with a Honda grill would be neither one nor the other.

Consider what happens when we begin to buy a car. We look at what is available, what features they include, and whether or not those features translate into advantages for us. We eliminate those beyond what we perceive to be our ability to pay for and maintain. We take each of those that remain and set up a mental scale with advantages on one side, and detractions on the other. This is the only point at which it makes sense to consider our like or dislike of the grill. Next we place each unit on a scale to see which packages are, in total, advantageous for us. Finally, we place the most advantageous package on the scale to see if the benefits we perceive outweigh the price we have to pay for the package. When it does, we buy a car.

If we buy a Chevy, it is because the complete package positively tipped all our mental scales. The grill was factored into our decision when we weighed the package. Being such an obvious and visible part of the car, there is no question it was noticed during our original investigation. So what happens if we now try to tell the world we don't like this grill and ignore the package concept that we did like?

Even though the grill design was only a partial factor in our decision to buy the car, we will now become disillusioned with what is in total, a satisfactory vehicle. We second-guess ourselves, leading others to believe we are less capable, less astute, or less intelligent than we really were when we bought this car. Even more destructive, we start the process of second-guessing ourselves, leading to diminution of the value we place on ourselves. When the accumulation of these stresses becomes too great, we may even discard a Chevy of considerable value to us, simply because we forget that it was a package we bought in the first place. This in itself can be self-demeaning, unless we were looking for a reason to unload the Chevy, and at some point become honest enough to admit that this was the reason for our choosing to seem illogical.

This sort of second-guessing can ruin relationships too. Consider yourself a young lady for a moment. You meet a well-mannered, attentive, and interesting young man who demonstrates his respect for you by being a gentleman. His only real drawback/deficiency, is his height. When you are in high heels, he is an inch shorter than you at your artificial height. When you put this person on the scales, on balance, he is a prince among men. So you buy the package and settle down to a warm and rewarding relationship. You discover that the young man is for real and all the admirable qualities you noted are genuine and are of value to you.

Until! There comes a day when a shopping spree presents you with a problem. You find just the shoes you've been looking for to go with your new dress. Only problem? They are four-inch spikes and you can't wear them when you're with your boyfriend because he is too short. At this point in time you can do one of two things. You can remember that it was a package that you bought, and as a package, your boyfriend is of great value. You will then put the shoes back or keep them to wear only on those occasions when you are alone. The alternative is to forget the benefits of the package and tell yourself that you are being denied these ideal shoes because of a deficiency in your lover. Let that thought smolder into resentment and prey on your valuable relationship until the poor man leaves the relationship, all the time wondering what he did to destroy something that seemed so good.

You lose because you lose him. He loses because he forfeits a relationship he obviously valued as seen in his treatment of you. Quite possibly his next girlfriend loses if he either doesn't trust her because of you, or he decides that treating women well only chases them away. Goodness knows, he probably has a covey of chauvinistic friends who will promote the concept rather than compete with a lady for this gentleman's attention.

All this becomes the sad result of forgetting what made you choose to associate with him in the first place. As a package he is valuable. His total package is valuable to you. Sure, the package may contain some negative aspects. Few things in this life are simplistic enough to have only plus characteristics, or even be limited to a few minus points. Like it or not, we are always accepting some of what we dislike, in order to gain a totality which is of value to us. Let's consider some other examples.

If you like your neighborhood and overall home, the only way to get a bigger back yard probably will involve moving from the home and surroundings you like.

If you like a magazine on cars, the only way that magazine could offer you articles on rock collecting would be to reduce the articles on cars which you do enjoy.

Homework is part of getting an education in a modern school environment.

Ice skating by definition requires ice, which has to be cold. For warm skating you can use roller skates. You just have to choose other places to skate. Also there is not as much excitement at competitive international levels, and you won't have the Ice Capades to advance to as a professional. The choice is yours.

Whatever you choose will be the best choice overall that you can make for you, at this point in your life, and under the total circumstances you find yourself to be in, at this time. Once you buy the package, keep the package. Enjoy the package. Always remember it is the package you bought and review it as a package. This will help you to be satisfied with your life and yourself here and now. You can still look forward and make a new decision if it is warranted, and if you have new information on which to base your new decision.

NEVER CHANGE YOUR MIND

Never change your mind. Only make new decisions based on new information. Changing your mind implies some defect in you or your thinking process. This can be denigrating to self-esteem. On the other hand, making a new decision based on new information makes sense and contributes to personal satisfaction and the building of self-esteem.

*****

ADDENDUM E
THE GESTALT PRAYER

I do my thing and you do your thing.
I am not in this world to live up to your expectations,
and you are not in this world to live up to mine.
You are you and I am I, and if by chance we find each other, it' s
beautiful.
If not. Too bad.

Frederick S. Perls

*****

-30-

INDEX

Printed in the United States
1418400004B/370-414